ORDER IN CHAOS

Objective and Key Results (OKR)

Kostiantyn Koptelov

Table of Contents

INTRODUCTION 5

ABOUT THE BOOK 10

HOW TO READ THIS BOOK 12

WHY DO YOU NEED TO SET GOALS? 14

Benefits of setting goals correctly 15

What new challenges arise while preparing the strategy 20

What new attitude should we have to set the goals? 24

Structure of new goal setting 28

So why are OKRs so good? 31

WHAT STANDS BEHIND OKR? 37

Basic principles, why should we know them. 38

Transparency 41

Should the goals be ambitious and what does that mean in OKR? 45

Timely or conscious goals 54

How do we create a roadmap 57

Why we try to avoid tiering up OKRs and benefits or performance review 61

Why do we need regular checkups? 76

Why do we reduce the number of goals? 78

Principle 30/70 80

How does the implementation of the principles work 81

HOW TO FORMULATE YOUR OKR CORRECTLY 84

Why it is important to formulate OKR correctly 85

What does OKR consist of? 88

OKR models and strategies 91

Steps for correct OKR planning 99

Checklist what is important to prepare in advance before formulating OKR for your team. 102

How to formulate a goal/objective 104

How to formulate Key Results 112

Examples of OKRs 130

Mistakes in the formulation of OKR 153

Checklist for OKR self-verification 155

WHAT TO DO NEXT 157

How to present your OKR to colleagues and team 158

What to do next with OKR inside your team 163

OKR TRACKING 166

How to track your OKR 167

Weekly OKR meeting 173

Monthly OKR meeting 176

GETTING MORE FROM YOUR OKR 179

What are the key thoughts to get more from OKRs 180

How to identify need and apply changes to your OKR 184

How to make a retrospective on your OKRs 186

HOW TO IMPLEMENT OKR IN A COMPANY 188

The purpose of OKR implementation 189

Gradual approach on OKR implementation 192

A step-by-step OKR implementation algorithm. 195

Common mistakes in OKR implementation 198

FINAL WORD 200

Introduction

With the passage of time and experience, I have come to realize that it is impossible to manage what one is not measuring. Management and decision-making are becoming more like trying to hit the finger in the sky if there is no measurement system.

And at critical moments, it begins to resemble a burning house, where people, not understanding each other, begin to save themselves without thinking about others. Project managers hate salespeople, and salespeople hate managers. Because of this, disagreements, denial, anger, and haggling between departments hurt the whole project. I have observed such situations more than once. And each time, my team and I found the right way to resolve it. Having gone through all these stages personally and having taught more than one stream of students and told them how to set up a management measurement system, I wrote this book.

More often than not, in these "burning" moments, you start implementing Key Performance Indicators (KPIs) or Objective and Key Results (OKRs), hoping that in a short period of time it will solve all the problems, and everyone will be fine. Too bad, but when you are looking for a wizard, you find a storyteller. Dreams of quick results soon turn into the realization that, as Warren Buffett said, "You Can't Produce a Baby in One Month by Getting Nine Women Pregnant." Change takes time.

When you begin to implement OKR, you must understand that it is a fairly lengthy process. And it cannot be done quickly because it requires a change in the habits of a large number of people and a paradigm shift in their thinking. Three quarters—that is about how long it will take before you see the first results. Implementing approaches to properly set goals and regularly track progress is a necessity. So be prepared that all your OKR activities will bear fruit in three quarters. Be patient, stock up on time, and keep your finger on the pulse. It is not a silver bullet, but this approach will definitely make a difference.

In this book, I will explain step by step what benefits we acquire when setting goals, what are the new approaches to planning in the current world, and the basic OKR principles, structure, and tools. I will pay special attention to the process of implementation and tell you about the most typical mistakes in it.

By reading this book, you will learn how to set and achieve your goals using the proven OKR method. This powerful method for setting goals has helped people and teams worldwide reach their full potential and achieve even more success.

Not only will you learn how to set and achieve your goals more effectively, but you will also learn how to do so in a way that maximizes your time and resources. The OKR method is designed to help you focus on what is most important and eliminate distractions, so you can make the most of your time and achieve more in less time.

In addition, this book will teach you how to organize your team around common goals using the OKR method. By ensuring everyone on your team is working toward the same goals, you can all be more productive and successful as a group. The OKR method is also a powerful tool for breaking through the glass ceiling and advancing your career.

This book is a good tool for directors, leaders, project managers, line managers, HR, and CEOs. I have organized the information about the implementation process in a way that makes sense and tried to answer the questions that often come up at all stages of OKR implementation. Here you will find everything you need to achieve the best results and avoid the mistakes that have already been made before you.

Important disclaimer. This is an extremely practical book. For more than five years, I have been talking about OKR and implementing it in different companies. During that time, I have concluded that in its pure form, the approach as described by the founders causes various interpretations and misapplications in different countries. The main reasons are different mentalities and different sets of basic skills. So, in this book, you will find an OKR that has been changed so that it can be used effectively and practically, taking as many cultural differences and ways of thinking into account as possible.

The examples in this book are often from the IT business field. This is done so because most of the audience reading this book is from outsourcing, engineering, or product businesses. The specifics force them to look for innovative approaches to management. But that does not mean that OKR is the province of programmers. I have implemented this approach in the real sector as well. I must say that it works very well there if the implementation is done correctly. Among the real sector clients were medical companies, boards of directors in the agricultural and fuel businesses, chain stores, plumbing equipment distributors, and even a chain of restaurants. Try the approach on yourself. And, if you have any questions, I am always in touch, such as on Instagram https://instagram.com/koptelov_org or https://www.linkedin.com/in/kkoptelov/

The process of writing and publishing a book is quite long, and the world is changing extremely fast. It is important for us to have time to adapt ourselves and our tools to these changes. So, my version of the OKR approach is constantly living and changing, getting better and more effective. If you are interested in staying abreast of the latest changes and trying the latest tools, I recommend you take an additional look at www.okr.how

So, don't let your goals remain just a dream—start reading this book and learn how to make them a reality with the OKR method. Take control of your life and career and achieve your goals today!

Disclaimer:

This book is meant to give you information, not legal advice, so don't take it that way. The information in this book comes from the author's research and personal experience, but it might not be complete or up to date. The use of brand names in this book is for illustrative purposes only and does not imply endorsement of or affiliation with the respective brand. The author and publisher make no promises or warranties, either express or implied, about the completeness, accuracy, reliability, suitability, or availability of the book or the information, products, services, or related graphics in it for any purpose. Any reliance you place on such information is, therefore, strictly at your own risk. In no event will the author or publisher be liable for any loss or damage, including, without limitation, indirect or consequential loss or damage, or any loss or damage whatsoever arising from loss of data or profits arising out of, or in connection with, the use of this book. If a brand name or trademark is mentioned in this book, it is up to the reader to get permission to use it.

About the book

Welcome to our class on setting OKR goals!

In this book, you'll learn why setting goals is essential and how to use the OKR method to reach them. We'll talk about why it's important to set objectives the right way and what can go wrong when planning. We will also talk about how important it is to change how you think about setting targets and how to set them using the OKR method.

You will also learn about the ideas behind OKRs, such as the importance of setting challenging goals and the need to set objectives with a purpose. We'll discuss how to make a roadmap and why avoiding tiering OKRs with decisions on employee bonuses and performance reviews is better. We will also talk about how important it is to make regular reconciliations and reduce the number of objectives.

Then, we'll talk about how to make your OKRs the best way possible, including what the structure and models of OKRs are and what the strategies are for formulating them. Here you will find some checklists to help you improve your OKR formulation process. Finally, we'll show you some examples of OKRs and discuss how to avoid common mistakes.

Next, we'll discuss how to present OKRs to your team and what to do next with them. We will also mention OKR tracking, including the OKR meetings that happen weekly and monthly.

Lastly, we'll talk about how to get more out of your OKRs, such as by figuring out where you can make improvements and doing retrospectives. We will also answer questions that are often asked about setting OKRs.

Thank you for joining us on this OKR Method journey to help you reach your goals. Let's get started!

How to read this book

The structure of the book is based on the OKR (Objectives and Key Results) method, which is a way to set goals that helps people and groups reach their goals. The book starts by talking about how important it is to set goals and what could go wrong if you don't do it the right way. It then introduces the OKR method and explains the ideas behind it, such as the importance of setting challenging goals and the need to set objectives with a purpose.

The book then delves into the specifics of how to use the OKR method, including the structure and models of OKRs and strategies for formulating them. The book has checklists and examples of OKRs to help readers improve how they come up with OKRs and avoid making common mistakes.

The book also covers how to present OKRs to a team and how to track progress, including OKR meetings that happen weekly and monthly. Finally, the book concludes by discussing how to get more out of the OKR method, such as by figuring out where improvements can be made and conducting retrospectives.

To get the most out of a book, you need to pay attention to what you're reading. This means taking notes, asking questions, and thinking about how the information relates to your own goals and objectives. This will help you better understand and retain the information, as well as make it easier to refer back to it later.

One effective approach is to read the book slowly and deliberately, taking the time to fully understand each concept and idea before moving on to the next. This may mean re-reading certain sections or pausing to think about how the information applies to your own situation. Additionally, it can be helpful to underline or highlight important points, or to make notes in the margins to remind yourself of key takeaways.

Another important aspect of reading the book effectively is implementing the techniques and strategies discussed in the book. This means taking action on the information you've learned rather than simply reading about it. For example, if the book is about the OKR method, it's essential to start formulating your own OKRs and using the method in your own work or personal life. This will help you better understand the method and see the results for yourself.

Finally, it is important to be patient with yourself as you learn and implement the OKR method, as it may take some time to fully understand and see results. Setting goals and working towards them is a process, and it's important not to get discouraged if you don't see immediate results. Instead, focus on making progress and celebrating small wins along the way.

Overall, reading this book effectively requires active engagement, implementation, and patience. By following these tips, you will be able to get the most out of the book and achieve your goals using the OKR method.

Why do you need to set goals?

Benefits of setting goals correctly

Why would you want to set goals?

This chapter is not just for you but for your team members as well. You, as leaders, most often understand why we set goals, but it often needs to be more evident to employees. You may hear from some: "Leave me alone; I have no time to deal with all this goal-setting stuff."

So, let's discuss why we set goals.

Have you heard of such a fascinating study from 1953 at Yale? They polled all of the graduates to find out what they had planned for their summer vacation and beyond.

About 3% of the graduates said they had specific plans that were formulated and written down.

About 13% said they understand what they want but haven't explicitly formulated or written anything down. They have an overall understanding, and that is enough.

84% of graduates said that they had experienced a difficult time studying there, and now they just want to rest and not set any goals.

Twenty years later, in 1973, they asked the same people again—everyone they could reach and find.

And it turned out that 84% of the graduates who hadn't set goals had achieved something. Their results were mediocre, but still there.

The 13% who had at least some formulation of goals but didn't write them down clearly achieved 80% more than the previous 84%.

And the last 3% achieved about 10 times as much as everyone else combined.

It is believed that this experiment was then repeated at Harvard in 1979.

How do you like this data?

The problem with this statistic is that, despite the fact that this study has received a lot of attention, Yale and Harvard have never confirmed that anything like this occurred.

When I heard that, I got a little upset. Super-inspiring data. I wonder if no one has ever done anything like that. So, I started looking. There had to be some scientific evidence to support setting goals.

And the Dominican University did a similar study. The results weren't as loud or as popular. They studied 267 people from 20 to 72 years old, completely different people from different locations and occupations.

They divided people into five groups: in the first group, they did not write down their goal; in the second group, they wrote it down; in the third group, they wrote it down and also made a plan of action in the direction of the goal; in the fourth group, they committed to a friend to achieve the goal; and in the fifth group, they agreed to write regular reports on progress towards the goal.

The result of this study is exciting. If you simplify things and divide the participants into two groups: those who set goals and those who did not, it turns out that those who didn't set goals reached half as many as those who actually did. Of course, the figures are not as loud as in the previous story, but this was a genuine scientific experiment.

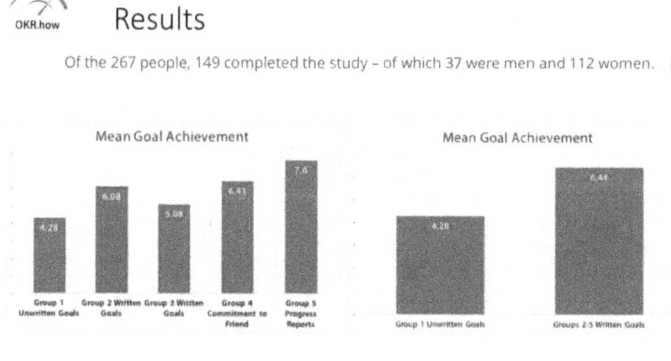

Results

Of the 267 people, 149 completed the study – of which 37 were men and 112 women.

©GAIL MATTHEWS / GOALS RESEARCH SUMMARY

It is crucial to write down your goals, make a public commitment, and report on them. In this case, you would get many benefits:

1. **Increased accountability.** When you tell people about your goals and how you're doing, they will hold you accountable for what you do. Because you don't want to let anyone down, this might help you stay focused and motivated.

2. **Support.** You can get help and support by telling people what you want to do and talking to them about your goals. Clarifying requests for help could be helpful if you need help from others to reach your goal.

3. **Increased motivation.** Reporting progress and sharing your goals with others help boost your motivation. Knowing that other people are aware of your objectives and are pulling for their achievement may increase your motivation to meet them.

4. **Increased likelihood of success.** Studies have shown that people who publicly declare their goals and put pen to paper are more likely to achieve them. Telling people about your goals makes you more focused and motivated.

Setting objectives in writing, being open about them, and reporting on them can help you be more accountable, get more support, be more motivated, and raise your chances of success.

So, let's sum up.

Setting goals can be an excellent way to focus your efforts, determine which tasks are most important, and track your progress. Having clear, specific goals can help you stay motivated and on track, as you have a clear target to work towards.

Goals can also help you make better decisions by giving you a sense of purpose and direction.

Setting goals and working towards them can also help you learn skills like managing your time, solving problems, and making decisions that can help you in both your personal and professional lives.

Lastly, reaching your goals can give you a sense of satisfaction and accomplishment, which can boost your confidence and sense of self-worth.

Setting goals can help you make the best use of your time, resources, and efforts and achieve the most important things.

What new challenges arise while preparing the strategy?

Several challenges can arise while preparing a strategy:

Lack of clarity. It can be easier to make a plan if you know your goals and objectives. With this information, making good decisions and putting together a plan is easier.

Limited resources. Another common challenge is having limited resources, such as time, money, or personnel. This can make it difficult to implement your strategy effectively.

Changing circumstances. The external environment can change quickly, disrupting your strategy. For example, you may need to change your strategy if the way your competitors act or your customers' decisions change.

Resistance to change. People often don't like change, which can make it hard to put a new plan into action. You may have to deal with resistance from stakeholders or employees if you want your strategy to work.

Limited visibility. It can take a lot of work to predict and plan for all the possible problems that could arise. This lack of visibility makes it hard to make a strong plan that considers all possible risks.

Overall, it can be hard to come up with a strategy because there isn't enough clarity, there aren't enough resources, things are constantly changing, people don't like change, and there isn't enough visibility. To make sure that your strategy works, you need to find and deal with these problems before they happen.

But why so?

A long time ago, we lived in a rather specific world where not much was changing, and one could plan for a decade or even more. But then came VUCA.

Volatility, Uncertainty, Complexity, and Ambiguity are all abbreviated as VUCA. It's used to define today's corporate climate, which is marked by quick change, complexity, and unpredictability. In a VUCA world, organizations need to be flexible, quick to change, and able to adapt to new situations.

VUCA is thought to have arrived in the 1980s with the start of the Cold War. But from the 2020s on, we've entered BANI with all the climate changes and pandemics.

BANI stands for Brittle, Anxious, Non-linear, Incomprehensible.

Brittle.

In the BANI universe, a system can look like it's working fine even if it's about to fall apart.
So, it's important to be careful and not put all your trust in operations, even if they seem reliable, flexible, and unbreakable.

Anxious.

The new oil is information, but too much of it leads to a severe issue: worry.
Even though we have the technology to help us make decisions, stress and anxiety will make us feel helpless and unable to make essential choices.

Nonlinear.

There is no longer any beginning, middle, or end in the current situation. At any point in the game, you must be ready to advance or retreat a few spaces.

Incomprehensible.

Lastly, the word "incomprehensible" means that people don't understand what is going on. They can't control it, understand it, or figure out what's going on and why. This means that they can't find the answers they're looking for, and if they do find answers, they can't figure out what they mean.

Why am I telling you all this?

Because when you're setting your goals, it's extremely important to consider the world that we're in. Here, in fact, we're talking about how to secure our planning in that fragile world.

We're talking about the fact that it will be essential for you to plan for extra contingency and an extra margin of safety in the goals you set out and in the resources, you allocate because the world is becoming brittle.

We need to be more empathetic to our employees and more conscious, especially of our safety in an anxious environment.

As the world is nonlinear, it becomes more and more vital for us to understand the context. Be aware of what's going on around us in order to not just do as written in some instructions or as told, but to understand why we're doing it and do it in the best possible way.

And, of course, if the world becomes incomprehensible, it's important for us to become clear and easy to understand.

What new attitude should we have to set the goals?

If I ask you to imagine a picture to illustrate strategic planning, you might think of a person sitting on a chessboard and thinking about some next step. But as you already know, everything is changing. In a BANI world, strategy turns into hockey. That is the game of high speed, high risk, and the inability to keep track of all the possible combinations.

Image by macrovector on Freepik

Strategy and planning themselves change, and we move from a world where we have clear plans to one where we need as much flexibility as possible.

Planning today is like driving a car in a fog.

When you sit behind the car wheel in fog, due to the fog lights of your car, you get a very clear view of some part of the road in front of you. You can see it as clearly as possible, but not for a long distance. And when we make some parallels with planning, you can see and plan very clearly for the quarter closest to you. So, it's clear, it's understandable, and everything is perfectly fine.

Further down this road, where our car fog lights are not so effective, everything is blurred; we see silhouettes; nothing is clear; but we can roughly guess what's next. So, some plans for the next quarter are foreseen, but not as clearly as one might wish.

Then there's deep fog; you can't see anything. And just ahead, poetically speaking, a guiding star is shining. Over a long distance, we know where we're going.

So, in terms of planning, you have a beacon goal that gives you the strategy and context; you have firm and clear goals for the first quarter and not too much in between.

We just got in to ride in the fog and enjoy the fog.

And now a few words when you are driving—you are not alone on the road in this fog. A company usually has more than one employee.

What do you think is the key to your safety on the road?

Quite right. Predictability. This is when you're predictable to others, and they're predictable to you.

The same is true in business. The predictability of what I do for the rest of the team is now critical. And, of course, the predictability of what other team members do.

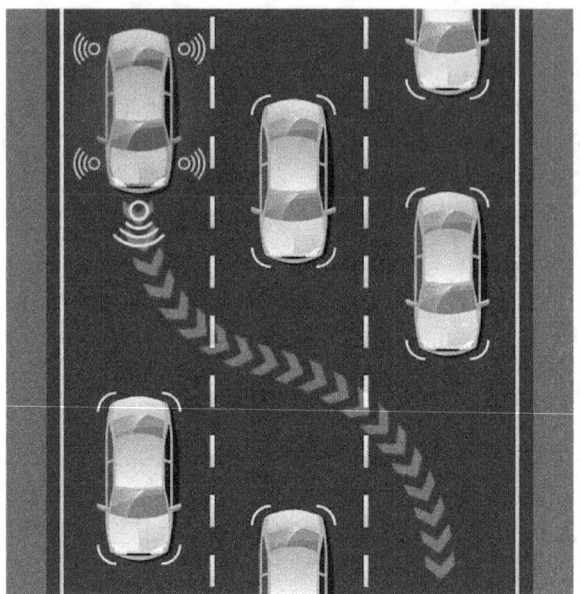

Image by jcomp on Freepik

As a result, regular synchronization and information exchange become critical in our modern world.

Let's sum up.

When planning now, we need to have a beacon goal, a clearly defined goal for the closest perspective, which is usually a quarter, and regular synchronization with other team members to achieve our destination.

ORDER IN CHAOS by Kostiantyn Koptelov

Structure of new goal setting

In this new world, we need a beacon, a guiding star, and some vision for the next 3 to 20 years. It's on a strategic level.

We need an understanding of where we want to get to in a year. It's such a benchmark; it's roughly where we want to get to in a year. This is the operational level.

We also need clear and specific goals for the nearest quarter at the tactical level.

And the next thing is a regular reality check—weekly reconciliations. We need them to achieve predictability. Where are we now in regard to our goals? Is our speed okay? Do we need any corrections? If someone on our team is lagging or if someone is speeding up, how should we adapt to reach our common goal?

These are the basic four things that we need when we are talking about planning in our new world.

So let's move on to the details.

We most often use BHAG-like goals at a strategic level. Big Hairy Audacious Goal. The only difference is that BHAGs are typically for 20 years or more, whereas we accept time horizons as short as three years. It depends on the company and the market it is in. BHAG is clearly understood and easy to grasp. It correlates with the company's core values. It's the beacon that I was talking about, the guiding star that shines for us and shows us where we are going.

Then we have the operational and tactical levels. Usually, that's the year and the nearest quarter. At this level, we use OKRs. They are clear, understandable, measurable, and inspirational.

Let's talk a little bit about the BHAG goal.

Why do we need it?
It discourages thinking too shallowly. When you set a long-term goal, which you yourself are a little afraid of, there is a sense of urgency and the need to hurry.

It helps build a great company. If your BHAG is "making it possible to explore and populate Mars," like Elon Musk's in his SpaceX project, then you realize that it can't be achieved if your company is mediocre.

It helps to hire A-people for the team. You'll want to hire the best people to achieve your BHAG. In addition, clarity and ambition will attract the right people who will want to participate in the realization of this goal.

Few BHAG examples:

1. "Put a computer on every desk in every home" – Microsoft.
2. "Any book, in any language, available in less than a minute" - Amazon
3. "Put a man on the Moon" – NASA
4. "Become a $125 billion company by the year 2000" – Walmart
5. "Crush Adidas" – Nike
6. "We will destroy Yamaha" - Honda

7. "Become Harvard of the West" – Stanford

There are four types of BHAG:

1. **Goal-oriented:** Establish an objective that is both quantitatively and qualitatively specified (e.g., "become a $125 billion firm by the year 2000"; Wal-Mart, 1990).
2. **Compete** against a common foe (Honda, 1970s): " We will crush Yamaha!"
3. Taking on the characteristics of a successful firm that isn't your direct rival ("Let's become a Nike of cycling" (Giro Sport Design, 1986)) is known as "**role-playing.**"
4. **Transformational:** Concentrated on changing the organization as a whole (e.g., "Let's convert this organization from a contractor into the most diversified high-tech business in the world"; Rockwell, 1995).

Let's sum up.

To have a working strategy, we need four elements: a BHAG-like goal on a strategic level, a yearly OKR, a quarterly OKR, and regular reconciliation and adaptation.

So why are OKRs so good?

What exactly are OKRs good for? What makes them so popular?

I will start with cases when companies come to me and say, "Let's implement OKR."

The most frequent cases are:
1. Companies that are preparing for growth and want not to lose manageability while scaling up.
2. Companies that grow up very fast and now their management is struggling.
3. Distributed teams that struggle to keep everyone united around common goals and values.
4. Creative teams (software development included), which are hard to manage with the help of classic instruments.

5. Companies that straddle the glass ceiling and are eager to achieve a new level.

I will talk about just a few cases from my more than 5 years of experience in OKR.

There was a software company that faced a glass ceiling. The company owner during the pre-project interview said, "We started about the same time as a few other companies, and another two companies started even later than we did. Now, these four are already way ahead of us, and we're still, well, at a good level: everything is still good with us, but it's like we're stuck". We started using OKR, and the company was able to open offices in new places and grow into new markets.

Another case. There was one of the IT companies that was leading in its geography. It was one of those companies where it is hard to say what they are doing. There was an outsourcing stream, and they had several projects that were not interrelated with each other. They had a problem in that every time they came up with a long-term plan, it was never put into action from year to year. Despite a significant amount of time spent developing the shared vision, everyone is pulling in their own direction. That's because everyone understands the company's vision in their own way. To make matters worse, the owner constantly interferes, assigning new tasks, priorities, and directions.

What have we managed to get with OKR in this case?

First and foremost, we committed to quarterly planning. It's fantastic because it reduces chaos for some companies that have new plans every day. At the same time, it makes businesses more flexible and helps businesses that are too slow to change out of their ruts. So, by fixing the planning by the quarter, we were able to solve the problem when everything changes in that company constantly.

In addition, we added the tracking and synchronization of these goals between projects' teams. This allowed us to have a better understanding of how our teams were working together and how their individual goals were contributing to the overall company goal. We were able to track progress and ensure that everyone was on the same page and working towards the same goal. It also helped us figure out where teams weren't working well together so we could fix the problems. This made it easier for teams to talk to each other and work together, which helped us reach our goals more quickly.

Let's talk about one more interesting case.

The creation of a startup within a rather large financial company to take advantage of a business opportunity. The startup team was made up of top managers who aimed to launch a product. The main strategy was to create a website to make themselves known loudly and attract potential customers. The marketing director of the parent company was involved in preparing marketing materials and organizing events to promote the website. Developers stated that the site would be ready in October. The marketing director started doing things to promote the business, like inviting bloggers, setting up events, finding places to hold them, holding giveaways, etc. It took a lot of effort to prepare everything for the site to start loud. So, after a while, the marketing director came to the developers two weeks before the October deadline and asked to show the site for testing. And got a surprise. They found out that there was some kind of "fire" at the parent company. And it was clear that if the parent company didn't have money, there was nothing for this startup to exist for. So, all the developers were assigned to fix the problem. There was no time for them to work on the website.

So, the marketing director came to me and said, "Konstantin, teach the developers how to set goals and finish them on time." And the technical director, the leader of developers, was sitting next to her and said, "You don't understand the nature of development." Well, that's the story.

We had a talk and realized that, in their particular case, it is unrealistic to set tasks for developers and expect them to be done right before the deadline. But that's not so terrible; startups should be agile at the end of the day. The real problem is that they found out too late about deadline shifts. So, we implemented a system of regular reconciliation. Short, structured weekly meetings revolved around clear and trackable goals. This gave them the ability to get information about the progress in time and adapt accordingly.

One more case. A distribution company that struggled with different departments having different understandings of what "growth" meant and how to achieve it. As a result, there was confusion and a lack of synchronization between departments. To solve this problem, we made sure that everyone worked toward the same goals and helped each other reach them by creating a set of unified goals and setting up clear, open communication and synchronization between departments.

There are many more of these success stories. So what I've given you now are stories from my practice. But there are also others:

1. Google – grew from a company of 40 employees to 60,000 employees.[1]
2. LinkedIn - become a $20 billion company in a limited time.[2]
3. Huawei - take their business success to the next level by boosting their business performance.[3]
4. Upserve - increased their employees from 30 to 80, hitting record sales of $1 billion.[4]
5. Revenue Grid – is building innovative software and inventing new markets using OKRs.[5]

So, let's summarize. Why OKRs are good:

1. OKRs add predictability.
2. Without loss of flexibility and adaptability.
3. They help to coordinate the work even if it is distributed and creative.
4. They help team members to understand what where, and when.
5. They stimulate to move towards the common goal.
6. And they are constantly improving the company, teams, and individuals by changing their mindset.

---

[1] https://www.managers.org.uk/knowledge-and-insights/article/how-does-google-get-things-done/

[2] https://firstround.com/review/the-management-framework-that-propelled-LinkedIn-to-a-20-billion-company/

[3] https://wma.my/business/huawei-gave-up-on-kpi-took-okr-to-reach-business-success-why/

[4] https://firstround.com/review/How-to-Make-OKRs-Actually-Work-at-Your-Startup/

[5] https://ain.ua/2022/11/24/chomu-okr-a-ne-kpi-dosvid-revenue-grid/

With OKR managers get:
1. Purposeful, coordinated teamwork.
2. Transparency in the work of the company, teams, and individual employees.
3. Increased focus and passion.
4. Focus on improvements, not just routines.
5. Increased quality of communication with employees.

All team members get:
1. Greater engagement. Employees see how their contributions impact the big goal.
2. Clarity of priorities. Everyone is clear about the company's goals and expectations.
3. Growth and development. In the process of OKR implementation, skill gaps can be identified, and a training plan can be created.

What stands behind OKR?

Basic principles, why should we know them.

OKRs may seem easy on the surface, but I've seen that they can be hard to effectively put into practice. In my experience, companies that try to rush the implementation process often struggle with OKRs and eventually decide to abandon them. I think this could be because of a lack of understanding or planning, and it's important to take the time to understand and use OKRs properly instead of trying to rush the process. I should also mention the importance of following principles in the implementation of OKRs. Why so?

Have any of you ever heard of a cargo cult? It's a thing that happens when people copy the actions and behaviors of others even though they don't understand the reasons behind them. This can lead to ineffective and even counterproductive results, as people are just going through the motions without a deep understanding of what they're trying to achieve.

To illustrate this concept, I'll give you an example from World War II. There was a group of natives living on a Pacific island where the Americans had built a military base. The natives saw that the Americans flew planes, talked on radios, and then got food and other supplies on a regular basis from some big iron bird. To the natives, these actions might have seemed like a ritual to please that big iron bird, and they might have thought that if they did the same things as the Americans, they would get the same benefits.

As a result, the natives built straw and wood replicas of American military equipment, such as planes, radios, and walkie-talkies. They even had shamans who pretended to be using these replicas to communicate with the gods or spirits, in the hope that this would bring them the same blessings as the Americans. They had turned all of this into a "cargo cult," copying what the Americans did without knowing what their actions stood for.

The point is that we don't want to turn our own organizations into "cargo cults" when we use management practices or approaches. Just copying the outside parts of a system or approach, like meetings, rules, or formats, without understanding the principles and motivations behind them can lead to more bureaucracy and inefficiency without actually getting the results that were wanted. Instead, it's important to take the time to understand the ideas and reasons behind the things we do so we can use them well and get the most out of them.

The main ideas behind OKRs are transparency, separating goals into those that are ambitious and those that are more realistic, focusing on a small number of goals, separating goals from evaluations and pay, measuring progress often, and finding a balance between setting goals from the top down and from the bottom up. By following these principles, we can make sure that our goals are clear, aligned, and attainable and that our progress toward those goals is regularly tracked and evaluated.

We are going to talk about these principles in the following lessons.

Principles

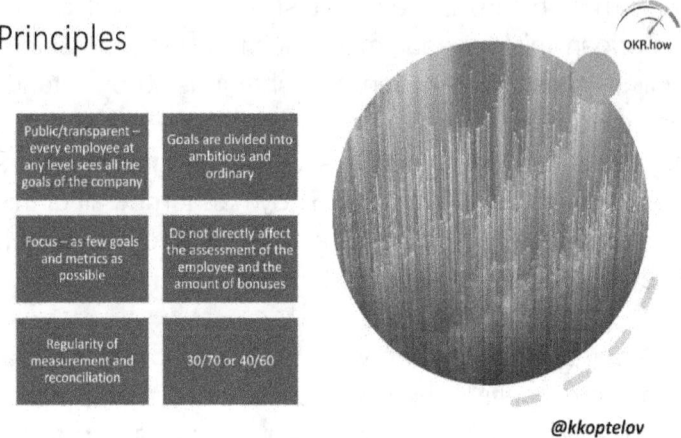

In addition to these principles, it's important to think about how the organization is aligned and how its parts depend on each other. By making sure that goals, expectations, and dependencies between departments are clear, we can make sure that everyone is working toward the same goals and that each department knows what it needs to do to help the organization reach its goals as a whole.

It's important to avoid becoming a "cargo cult"—blindly mimicking what other companies do without understanding the underlying principles. By following the OKR method's values and principles, we can move toward our goals, grow, and be successful in the long run.

Transparency

The first and basic principle of the method is publicity and transparency. Thanks to free access to information, each employee can see what others are doing, what tasks need to be completed, and how to adjust the schedule to accommodate interdependent tasks.

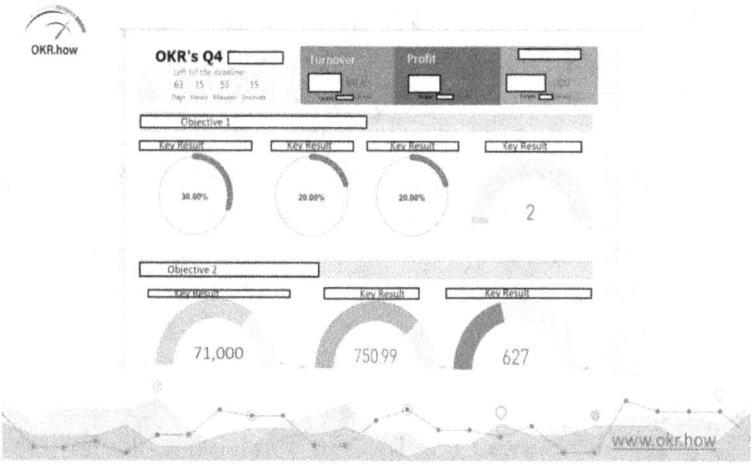

What justifies such an open approach?

First, it adds motivation. There are two types of motivation: "carrots in the front and carrots in the back" (positive and negative motivation). In this case, we get both types of motivation by having everyone see how their goal relates to the goals of others and the main goal of the company. This makes sense: doing more meaningful work always feels good; it gives more motivation.

Second, accountability. Transparency allows anyone to control everyone. Your tasks are connected; we are swimming in the same boat, and you see who is rowing and who is not. You are not reporting to management, to whom you can send a rearranged version of last year's report, but to those with whom you work, to your colleagues. In some cultures, it's a common belief that "the boss is a fool." That's another reason to report to your colleagues. They see what you do, and they are harder to deceive because they can always control you just as much as you control them. It's also important to realize that when we report to our colleagues, we are automatically in sync. When, for example, the marketing staff, who have one of their goals to bring clients to the site, hear that the development department doesn't plan to work on the site this week, they have a chance to adjust their plans and prioritize other tasks for the current week. And they won't need additional calls or meetings to do so.

Additionally, publicity and transparency create context. Any task assigned can be handled differently with different approaches. By understanding why you were assigned the task, you can solve it in the most effective way.

When you write code for a program to be used on a test server, you do it effortlessly; you just do your job well. But when you realize that you're doing a task that will become part of something bigger, you instinctively take a different approach to your work. You write scalable code where you have different tables, structures, and code architectures. There's also the opposite case, where the code you're writing is used only to test and show off what it can do. Then you'll take the easiest and fastest approach to writing it. Understanding and seeing the whole process gives you a different, more productive approach to your work.

In this way, publicity and transparency create context and overall accountability. Everyone is in plain sight, so employees perform and get results as close as possible to what is expected of them.

There was an interesting case in my practice to illustrate this principle.

The owner of a chain of restaurants is a very charismatic person. He is very quick to fire up ideas. His employees are afraid of him. So once we sit down with him and have a regular talk, he comes up with some kind of idea. He calls HR and says, "Let's make an employee group on Facebook."

After a while, he asks HR about that task. What do you think was done?

Yes, HR created a group on Facebook and invited all the employees there.

Do you think the owner was satisfied with that? No.

Why? The owner did not want the group. He ran a chain of restaurants in different parts of the country, and he wanted a way to quickly talk to all of his employees. In that particular case, less than 20% of the employees were using Facebook. So a lot of time was wasted to make a group, invite people, motivate them to use it, and prepare content. And at the end of the day, the group was stillborn; almost no activity was observed there. But if there were a public dashboard,

HR would be able to understand the sense of the task, the context, and maybe use another tool that would be better for that particular company at that moment in their evolution.

Let's summarize.

Having goals that are clear and publicly available to employees can help make sure that all team members know what the company's goals are and can work towards them. It can also help to create a sense of shared purpose and solidarity within the organization.

There is only one thing to watch out for: not all goals should be made public if they contain sensitive information that shouldn't be widely known.

Should the goals be ambitious and what does that mean in OKR?

You have to be very careful here. The books say that all OKR indicators should be ambitious and unattainable. And I say that you have to adapt this principle to the culture of a particular company. Sometimes ambition is relevant, and sometimes an ordinary, achievable goal is enough.

Why is this the case? I will explain it with the help of a picture.

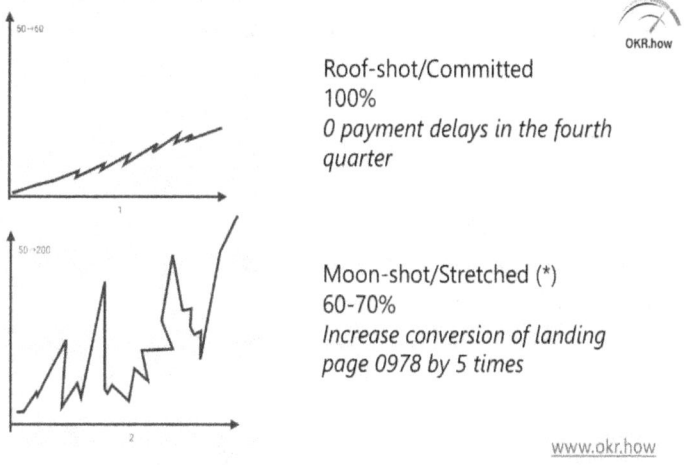

Roof-shot/Committed
100%
0 payment delays in the fourth quarter

Moon-shot/Stretched (*)
60-70%
Increase conversion of landing page 0978 by 5 times

www.okr.how

A typical goal setting is depicted in the figure above. We start with an indicator that we regularly achieve.

For example, create 50 new features in the case of the IT business, and create 50 products per quarter in the case of manufacturing. And so, having learned that the goals should be ambitious, management sets us a goal of making 50 + 20 more new features in a quarter.

Let's assume the goal is achievable and quite realistic. But how do we accomplish it? This can be done in three ways:

The first way is to reduce quality. For us, this is unacceptable. And for those who think it's okay, it's not profitable because work done carelessly will need to be redone and will cost more to help customers, market, and deal with negative feedback.

The second way is to increase the amount of work. Increase the volume and work longer to achieve the goal. Hire additional employees, introduce extra shifts, and work overtime.

Method three: improve and optimize the process. Most likely not radically, because big changes always run the risk of going wrong because the new way doesn't take hold or because it runs into resistance or technical problems. All the time that should have been spent working was spent on the process of change and readjusting.

The second and third ways are more or less adequate.

When we talk about goals being ambitious and unachievable within the OKR approach, the task sounds different: to do not 50 functions a month, but 200! That is not 10–20% more but dramatically more—that is several times more. And the difference here is not only in quantity but also in the understanding that it is impossible to achieve more by doing everything the old way. I never get tired of repeating: "Ambitious goals can only be achieved by ambitious actions."

With a goal of 200 realized functions per quarter, it will not work as in the previous example:

1. Hiring more employees won't work. First, the labor market won't always allow us to hire four times as many people as quickly. Second, it's not so easy because, for 7 new people, we have to hire an extra manager, which is more difficult and expensive. And then there is the question of economic feasibility.

2. Some kind of reliable improvements, most likely, will not allow a fourfold increase in performance. Here, it is probably necessary to take a risky path rather than a reliable and predictable one.

What to do?

Thinking outside the box.

To reach such a super-goal, you have to do something new and different. To repeat, "ambitious goals can only be achieved in an ambitious way."

We set ourselves stretched goals in areas where we need breakthroughs. We shouldn't use this method if all we need to do is a little more than usual.

But there are even sadder uses for ambitious goals. One can encounter such cases where owners think along the following lines:

"My employees are making 50 units now, and I need 100. If I say to them, "Guys, I need 100," they will make 70. So, I'd rather give them the figure 200, and then we start haggling, and we agree on 150 units. "They will undoubtedly do 100 as a result."

What is wrong with this approach? It leads to discounting the goal and achieving average results. People quickly get used to the idea that if a manager says 200, it means 100.

To avoid this, you need to act with a clear understanding: if we set an ambitious goal, we want to get it all, all 200 units. That is, in the process of moving toward the goal, we do not think that "it would be good to achieve something." We are determined to achieve that goal in its entirety. That means that we need to constantly review how we are trying to achieve it. Remember, "It is only possible to achieve ambitious goals in an ambitious way."

It is also important not only to set such an ambitious goal but also to check it off in the process of achieving it. If the goal is ambitious, every week you need to ask yourself, "Buddy, how are you achieving it?" Because the answer, "I'm trying really hard," is another cognitive distortion because we get used to the rut. And over time, we get tired and go back to the usual solutions and operations. At first, you may be motivated by big goals, but after a week or two, you may go back to your old ways and habits without even realizing it. But in this way, it is impossible to achieve a new goal that is many times greater than the previous one. And if we do not achieve it, we will be demotivated by failure. To prevent this from happening, we regularly ask the question, "How do you go about reaching your goal?" If trying to achieve the goal still looks like a rolling path, then we think, experiment, and do things differently.

When we talk about being ambitious and unattainable, we are primarily talking about the fact that we are working toward these goals, not by some improvement in processes or tools, not by increasing the amount of work or the number of hands, but by looking for something radically new: previously unprecedented experiments for ourselves and the project.

Please note that it's very important not to get into a "60–70% mistake." Maybe you've heard that it is okay to achieve your ambitious goal for 60–70% of it. This means that your goal was ambitious enough. The problem here is that sometimes people start to perceive 60–70% as the new 100%. So, they do some basic math in their minds and start aiming to get not 100% of the set goal but 60–70% of it. And they lose one of OKR's superpowers. Why is this important? Let me tell you a very interesting story.

There was a scientific experiment about which I was told during one of my training sessions. One woman raised her hand and told me that story. I couldn't find proof that that experiment worked, so please think of it more as an example than as real scientific data.
So, scientists were doing an experiment. They took a hound and an athlete. From what they've figured out, this hound and this athlete are mechanically similar when it comes to running short distances. Something like: a hound has four legs, but an athlete's legs are longer; a hound has strong muscles, but an athlete has a bigger pace; etc. Theoretically, because they are the same mechanically, as per the scientists' calculations, they should finish simultaneously. But of these two, there was always someone who finished first. Who do you think was always first? A hound. But why?

It was not aware of where to stop.

So, I need to bring up the concept of "the finish line effect," where people tend to slow down as they approach their goals. This effect is often called the "goal gradient," and it has been seen in many different situations, such as running and making decisions, as well as in other psychological processes.

One possible explanation for this effect is that it shows a basic principle of motivation: as we get closer to our goals, the reward or outcome becomes more real and immediate, which can make us less motivated to keep going. This is known as "satiation," and it can cause people to slow down or reduce their effort as they approach a goal.

It's also worth considering that there may be other factors at play in this phenomenon. For example, people may slow down as they approach a goal because they are feeling exhausted or burned out, or because they are experiencing negative emotions like anxiety or stress. Additionally, people may simply be more cautious or risk-averse as they get closer to a goal and may be less likely to push themselves as hard.

Overall, it's important to realize that this "finish line effect" is common and to take steps to deal with it in order to maximize performance and reach lofty goals. This could mean, as you said, setting more difficult or aspirational goals or finding ways to keep yourself motivated and on task as you near the end of a task or project.

One more problem here is perfectionism syndrome. It might be tempting to lower your goals to get more done, but it's important to think about what might happen if you do that. In some cases, lowering your goals may lead to a sense of accomplishment and progress as you are able to achieve more of your goals more quickly. However, it's also possible that this approach could lead to a lack of motivation and a sense of complacency, as you may not feel challenged or motivated to push yourself to achieve more.

It might be better to find a balance between setting goals that are both realistic and hard enough to push you to grow and get better. This can help keep you motivated and give you a sense of progress while keeping you from falling into the traps of perfectionism.

If you have problems with being a perfectionist, it might help to work with a coach to find ways to handle and deal with these problems.

Let's summarize.

Putting goals into two groups, "ambitious" and "normal," can help you set priorities and use your resources well. The most challenging or aspirational goals are the most ambitious ones, and they may take more time, work, or money to reach. On the other hand, ordinary goals are those that are easier to reach and more likely to be done in a shorter amount of time.

By dividing goals in this way, it can be easier to focus on the most important or impactful goals first while still making progress on the smaller, everyday tasks that need to be completed. This can help make sure that the organization is making steady progress toward its overall goals while still leaving room for flexibility and adaptability.

It's important to keep in mind, however, that all goals should be aligned with the overall mission and values of the organization, and that resources should be allocated in a way that is consistent with these priorities.

Avoid these general mistakes:
1. Setting ambitious goals as usual achievement +20-30%. Goals between ordinary and ambitious are not working at all. Use whether ambitious or ordinary, avoid everything between this.
2. Perceiving 60-70% as new 100%.
3. Moving towards ambitious goals as towards usual.
4. Not reminding yourself and others that "ambitious goals can be achieved only using ambitious strategies".

Timely or conscious goals

It seems that we essentially have two types of goals and two types of planning, if you will. One approach is focused on time, where we start with a fixed time frame and then try to fit our goals and actions into that time frame. This can be useful for creating structure and focus, but it may also limit our options and creativity, and it may not allow for much flexibility or room for adjustment.

The other approach is focused on meaning and purpose, where we start with a meaningful, challenging goal and then work backwards to determine how much time we need to achieve it. This approach allows for more flexibility and creativity, and it can be more inspiring and motivating as it allows us to focus on what is most meaningful and important to us. But it may be harder to plan and carry out because we may need to put in more time and effort, and it may be harder to track our progress and change our strategy as needed.

So, what do we do if we want to set conscious rather than timely goals?

1. Think about what the new quality is you want to earn. But don't go too far. For example, we were a distributing company and now want to become a full cycle company. Or we were doing our work well and now want to become the most automated department.
2. Formulate a short description of the new state. No more than one sentence.
3. Ask yourself and a team, what is the realistic timeline for this state to be achieved.

4. Brainstorm how it is possible to achieve this goal in a year or quarter. For example, we were making 50 new features a year, now want 200. How can we achieve this? We can buy another company, we can become an open-source product, we can switch from hiring people in the office into working with freelancers.

Any goal can be achieved in almost any time frame. The only question is: What should we become? Or what abilities do we need to acquire in order for that to happen?

One disadvantage of setting goals based on time is that they may not be very motivating. For example, if you set a goal to swim 100 meters in 90 seconds, it may not be very inspiring or exciting. It may not give you a strong emotional or physical reaction, and it may not feel like a significant achievement.

Another disadvantage of setting time-based goals is that they may be the result of compromise. This means you may have looked at your previous performance and added a round number to your goal instead of setting a truly challenging or meaningful target. This can lead to goals that are not well-defined or meaningful, and it can be difficult to explain why you have set a particular goal or why you have not been able to achieve it.

In contrast, setting goals based on meaning or purpose can be more motivating and inspiring. For example, if you set a goal to swim the Bosporus, which is at least 6.5 kilometers, it may be a much more exciting and meaningful goal. It may be more inspiring to your friends and family, and it may give you a stronger emotional or physical reaction. It's clear why

I can't swim 6 kilometers or less, and it's a much more impressive achievement to talk about.

So, setting a goal to swim the Bosporus is a much more meaningful and inspiring goal than setting a goal to swim 100 meters in a certain time. The Bosporus goal is clear and concrete, and it is easy to understand whether you have achieved it or not. It is also realistic and achievable, although it may take a year or a year and a half to train for it. On the other hand, the goal of swimming 100 meters in a certain time may not be as motivating, as it is just a number for the sake of a number. It could also be a compromise instead of something meaningful or inspiring. In addition, such a goal may lack flexibility, as it only allows you to swim in a specific way and in a specific place. In contrast, the Bosporus goal allows for more flexibility and creativity in terms of how you train and prepare for it. Overall, it is important to set goals that are meaningful and inspiring, rather than just numbers or targets that lack significance.

Overall, the choice between setting time-based goals versus meaning-based goals will depend on your personal preferences, company culture, and circumstances. It may be helpful to experiment with both approaches and see which one works best for you.

How do we create a roadmap

Creating a roadmap to achieve your goals can help you stay on track and make progress towards your objectives. There are two main approaches to building a roadmap: the linear approach and the flexible approach.

The linear strategy is to break your goal into smaller pieces that are easier to handle and then work on each one in a systematic way. If you want to buy a car, for instance, you might start by accumulating money for a down payment, looking into several models, and haggling with a seller. Because it offers a clear path to follow and helps keep you organized and focused, this strategy may be successful. In this case, we usually determine a goal for the year, and then it is simple to establish goals for the quarter. Every quarter's goal would be one-fourth of the annual goal.

The second way to make a goal roadmap is to start with the reason or motivation for the goal and then figure out the best and most efficient way to reach it. It doesn't start with the initial goal statement. For example, if your goal is to have a car, you start asking yourself why you need one. There could be a number of reasons for this, such as prestige, ease of use, the ability to go far, and the chance to go as fast as possible. Then, before the start of this quarter, you could evaluate all of the available transportation options and select the one that best meets your needs and resources. Then do it again in the next one. So, in the first quarter, you may choose to skate; in the next, to bike; and so on. Every quarter, you achieve your real goal—to move faster, for example. The main difference is that in this approach, you get what you really need every quarter, not just at the end of the year as in the previous one. This method is better for changing situations because it lets you be flexible and change your plan as needed instead of being stuck on one path.

Let's talk about some examples.

Let's imagine that we are working for an IT outsourcing company. We are planning the year and understand that we want to achieve a certain amount of profit, gross margin, and head count this year. And then we split the metrics into quarters, so that in every quarter we expect to reach some figure, usually 1/4 of the yearly goal.

When we want to use an agile approach, we start by trying to understand what we really want to achieve beyond those figures. Let's say we want to be the number-one IT outsourcing company. And when we think about plans for a quarter, we ask ourselves, "How can we become the leader in this quarter already?" Okay, let's move gradually. In the first quarter, we want to be the leader in Ukraine. In the second quarter, we want to become a leader in Europe. In the third quarter, we want to be the best in Latin America. And in the fourth quarter, we are the world leader. So, in each quarter we are going towards what we really want: leadership, not just taking small steps toward a larger goal.

One more example.

One day, a person came to me for personal coaching on setting goals. They told me that their goal was to make $1,000,000 per year and reach that goal within five years. We began to discuss this goal in terms of the amount of money that would be earned each year, with the idea that each year's earnings would be a step towards the ultimate goal of $1,000,000 per year. The first step was to start earning $100,000 per year, then $200,000, then $400,000, then $800,000, so the final year would be finished with $1,000,000 earned.

However, as we went through this process, I had the feeling that something wasn't right. So I asked the person how they felt about making $100,000 per year. They responded that they thought it was a good goal, but as we continued to talk, it became clear that there was no spark. I repeated the question regarding next goals, and only when we came to $1,000,000 did I see a twinkle in their eyes. So there was a big risk of failure as they would need to slog on for 5 years without any certain winnings.

I asked the person why they wanted to make $1,000,000 per year and what they hoped to achieve with that kind of income. They hesitated at first, but eventually admitted that they wanted to be seen as successful and "good fellows" by their friends, who were already millionaires. This helped me see that the real reason for wanting to reach the goal wasn't money, but rather a desire to be popular and accepted by others.

I told her that it would probably take a lot of hard work and discipline to reach this goal, and that it might be hard for most people to keep up that level of effort for five years without some extra motivation. I explained that professional athletes and military personnel might be more likely to be able to accomplish a goal like this due to their strong willpower and discipline, but that for most people, it might be more realistic to plan in a more agile way, from victory to victory.

They agreed, so we started thinking about how to draw a roadmap, not in terms of chunks but by splitting the way into spots with clear winning points on each. As we found out that the person wanted to be "a good fellow," which means to be a millionaire, we started thinking about how they could become a millionaire in the first year. So we invented another roadmap: 1,000,000 hryvnias (the Ukrainian currency) in the first year, 1,000,000 Hong Kong dollars in the third year, 1,000,000 Australian dollars in the fourth year, and finally $1,000,000. Gradations were based on the difference in exchange rates.

When making goals for a roadmap, it is important to see a "twinkle in their eyes," which shows that they are excited about the goal and want to reach it. People who are enthusiastic and passionate about their goals are more likely to be motivated and devoted to accomplishing them. This can improve the odds of success and make the process of working towards the goal more enjoyable. Seeing the "twinkle in their eyes" can also help encourage and motivate people who are helping set goals by creating a positive and exciting atmosphere.

Why we try to avoid tiering up OKRs and benefits or performance review

We have previously addressed the key principles that guide our decisions in OKR. Now, I want to focus on a topic that has garnered a lot of attention: the connection between OKRs (objectives and key results) and pay or grading.

Why do we avoid linking these three elements? The answer lies in the way organizations often approach motivation and pay. When we face challenges or have a lot on our plates, it is tempting to look for a quick fix. We want to find a magician that will give us a single tool for setting goals, tracking progress, evaluating employees, and determining the amount of bonuses. Unfortunately, more often than not, when we look for a magician, we just find "storytellers" who provide temporary relief but do not address the root cause of the issue. As a result, they do not work in the long run.

We want to talk about the main difficulties and dangers that arise when we try to link pay and grading to performance goals. By knowing about these problems, we can make better decisions about how to keep our employees motivated and pay them fairly.

In any company, there are three types of activities:
1. Innovative,
2. Routine or operational,
3. Observational.

Innovative activities are those that are new and have not been done before by the company. These can be risky and difficult to predict in terms of cost and timeline. Routine activities, on the other hand, are those that are already established and have clear instructions, standards, and measurement tools. Observational activities just involve watching, so you can't do the other two types of activities at the same time.

Point 1. Where there is money, there is attention.

When it comes to earning money, the company almost always relies on routine activities. This is true in most cases because innovative activities are uncertain and unpredictable, and therefore it is difficult to accurately predict how much money will be made from them. Routine activities, on the other hand, are easier to plan for and more stable. This makes them a more reliable way for the company to make money. Only when you charge three to four times the cost of production or when innovative activities become established routines can you earn money from them.

If the company is earning money on some kind of activity, we can say that most attention would be drawn to such activities. So, if we want to tie employee payments to some activities, we would start with routine ones as they are easier, considered more fair by the staff, and are economically reasonable.

Point 2. Creative tasks are hardly tracked.

It is generally more effective to track Key Performance Indicators (KPIs) for routine activities, as they are more predictable and have clear goals and reference points. This allows for more accurate measurement and tracking of performance. On the other hand, innovative activities may be harder to track with KPIs because they may involve experimentation and have less predictable results. Observational tasks don't involve taking part in the work process, so it wouldn't make sense to track them with KPIs.

So as we track routine activities, more attention will be drawn to them.

Point 3. In real life we give low priority to unclear tasks.

Let's imagine you give your subordinates two tasks: urgent and important. What do you think they would choose to do first?

When I ask this question in my lectures, the most common answer is "urgent."

But this is a tricky question, because usually people start with the tasks that are clearer to them. When employees have a clear understanding of what is expected of them and how to complete a task, they are more likely to prioritize and complete it effectively.

If we return to our model, when we have three types of activities: innovative, routine, and observational, which type of task do you think is usually more clear? Of course, routine tasks are easier because you know what to expect because you don't do them the first time you get instructions.

It's a running joke that people hate only two things: routine and things that disrupt their routine.

Point 4. People love innovations only in words.

There is a study that suggests that there are two types of activity: creative activity and routine activity. Creative work requires you to think more and come up with new ideas, while routine work is more mechanical and involves doing the same thing over and over again. The research found that when money is used to motivate creative tasks, it can actually decrease motivation and performance. This is because creativity is often driven more by the desire to do something for its own sake than by rewards from the outside world. When people are motivated by things like money that come from the outside, it can make them less interested in doing the task for its own sake. This can result in lower creativity and lower-quality work.

On the other hand, money can be a good way to motivate people to do routine tasks that don't require as much creativity. Since these tasks don't depend as much on internal motivation, money might be a better way to get people to do them.

But people may be more motivated to do creative work if they get something other than money, like praise, recognition, or a sense of accomplishment. These kinds of rewards can help people feel more motivated on their own, which can lead to better performance and more creative ideas.

If we go back to our model, which tasks do you think are creative and therefore less effectively stimulated by monetary motivation when we have three types of activities: innovative, routine, and observational? Of course, they must be innovative.

Point 5. Linking pay and performance appraisal to achievement of goals may lead to a situation where only those goals that are paid for will be pursued.

Monetary motivation can lead to problems when people start avoiding doing things they don't get paid for.

I'll give you a story that illustrates this point. There was an old man who lived alone in an apartment complex and was fed up with the noise from children playing soccer beneath his windows. In an effort to stop the racket, he approached the children and offered to pay them to continue playing. He started with $10 for a game. Initially, the children were excited about getting paid, and their performance improved. However, in a week, the man came to them and told them that he should reduce the amount of money to $5 per game as he had some financial troubles. The children's motivation and performance declined. And when, in the third week, he came and said that he was not able to pay the children for a game, they stopped playing. They considered that it would not be fair for him to enjoy the game for free. Even if the activity was enjoyable at first, monetary rewards can make people less motivated and less good at it.

We lose the ability to change and come up with new ideas, and we lose our striving for innovation and change. In this case, the only thing that works as a motivator for businesses is money. I've been in this situation; a number of very large and serious companies came to me for help with similar issues. They were feeling as if they were up against a glass ceiling. They were trying to start some new activities and projects, some innovations, but the executives don't want to do them if they don't get paid extra for additional tasks. The company was ossified.

And even more—all that creativity that used to be channeled into work can now be channeled into playing with numbers.

I want to illustrate this point with a case I observed. There is a company that conducts clinical trials for new medical drugs. In these trials, the drugs are tested on patients to find out if they are safe and effective and if they have any side effects. The company has a specialty called a clinical research associate (CRA), whose job is to visit medical facilities and ensure that the studies are being conducted according to protocol and ethical standards. This is similar to a project manager in a standard business, who makes sure that projects are carried out according to regulations and company policies. If there is a problem, the CRA must document it and resolve it in a way that does not compromise the integrity of the data or the patients' safety. Some problems were easy to resolve, but unfortunately, there were a lot of them that were not resolved for months.

The company implemented a system in which the amount of bonuses given to employees was determined by the closing rate of problems. This caused the closing rate to go up a lot in the first two months, but it also led to employees cheating the system to get the numbers they wanted. For example, they might have made up data or rushed to finish projects before all the problems were fixed. This can compromise the quality of the work being done and ultimately harm the company's reputation and bottom line.

Point 6. The problem of different units of measurement.

When setting goals, it is common to use systems of calculation and measurement to determine how to achieve them. For example, a company may want to make $5,000,000 and set specific goals for the number of active users, the amount of money each user makes, and the number of times a software product is installed. However, these calculations and measurements are often based on hypotheses about how different values will convert into one another, and in reality, these conversions may not always be accurate.

As a result, we can anticipate a situation in which individual goals are met at a 90–120% level but overall company goals are met at a 50–60% level only.

This can also mean that goals have to be recalculated and changed all the time, which can be confusing if the previous metrics were tied to bonuses. So, people can resist change, as any changes would affect their safety in terms of money and career.

Point 7. Local maximum problem.

If we directly link money and appraisal, we can expect "local maximum problems."

"Local maximum problem" is a term used in business to describe a situation in which a department or team is focused on maximizing its own performance indicators instead of thinking about the overall success and efficiency of the company. This can make the company less balanced and less efficient, which can hurt its performance. For example, if one department is working very hard to maximize its output, it may lead to overproduction in that department, while other departments may not be producing enough to meet demand. This can create bottlenecks and waste and ultimately harm the company's overall performance. Businesses need to find a good balance and make sure that all of their departments are working together to make the company successful.

Also, the local maximum problem can make departments fight with each other because they are all trying to improve their own performance indicators. This can create a toxic work environment and lead to a breakdown in teamwork and collaboration. To get the best results, businesses need to find ways to encourage teamwork and cooperation instead of competition.

Point 8. It is virtually impossible to reliably determine what contribution a particular employee has made to overall success.

The world is changing and evolving, and as a result, the systems and structures that we rely on are also changing. One big change that is happening is that mechanical and analytical systems are giving way to organic systems.

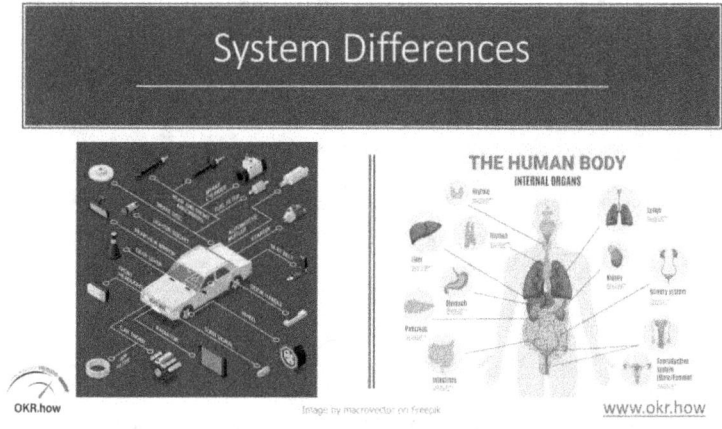

Mechanical and analytical systems are those that can be easily broken down into their individual parts and studied separately. A good example of this is a car, where each component can be taken apart, examined on its own, and then reassembled to function as before. These kinds of systems are easy to understand and use because the connections between the parts are clear and easy to see.

On the other hand, organic systems are made up of many interconnected parts that cannot be easily separated and studied individually. A good example of this is the human body, which is made up of countless cells, tissues, and organs that all work together to keep the body functioning properly. Because everything is connected and depends on everything else, it is much harder to figure out what each part or component does and how it fits into the whole.

This move toward organic systems can make it hard to understand and keep a sense of justice, especially in the business world. When it is more difficult to understand the specific contribution of each person or team in a company to the overall goal, it becomes harder to fairly award credit and compensation. Also, improving one part of the system, like getting rid of an employee who doesn't seem to be needed, can have unintended effects on the efficiency and success of the company as a whole. Businesses need to be aware of this shift toward organic systems and figure out how to work with them if they want to stay successful and fair.

To summarize the possible dangers of tiering goals to appraisal and payments.

1. Focusing on routine tasks and using monetary incentives to motivate employees can lead to a decline in innovation and stagnation of the company, as well as the loss of employees with innovative capabilities.
2. Monetary incentives may be effective in motivating employees to focus on routine tasks, but may not be sufficient to motivate innovative tasks.
3. When employees are given Key Performance Indicators (KPIs) to track, they may try to manipulate the system to achieve the desired numbers, rather than focusing on the quality of their work.

4. Using significant monetary rewards as incentives may result in falsified results.
5. Tracking KPIs for individual employees may lead to competition and reduced teamwork among units or teams within the company.
6. We can totally unbalance the company having local maximum trouble.

How to solve this problem.

In business, it is important to have a system in place for motivating and rewarding employees. However, traditional methods of tying employee pay directly to performance indicators, such as OKRs (Objectives and Key Results), may not always be effective. Instead, it's important to have separate systems for judging how well employees do their jobs, figuring out how much they should be paid, and coordinating work. These systems should not be directly tied to one another, as they serve different purposes and have different definitions of fairness.

So, we need three subsystems:
1. the performance appraisal system,
2. the compensation system,
3. the work coordination system.

Each of these systems has its own problems and limits, and they should be handled separately to make the workplace feel fair.

The performance appraisal system is in charge of figuring out how much an employee has helped the company. This can be done through regular performance reviews, setting specific personal development goals and objectives, and providing feedback on an ongoing basis.

The compensation system is responsible for determining how much an employee is paid. Money isn't always what drives people to work, and relying too much on the pay system can be ineffective. It's important to think about each employee's unique needs and motivations and find the right balance between these three systems to create a motivating and productive workplace.

The work coordination system is in charge of making sure that employees work well and efficiently together. This can be done through clear communication, setting roles and responsibilities, and giving support and resources as needed.

When we talk about OKR, this is solely a work coordination system. To avoid all of the issues raised previously, we do not make payment and appraisal decisions directly from OKR.

In this example, we can consider the car as a resource or employee assigned to the task of bringing us from Kyiv to Odesa. We have set clear goals for the task, including the time it should take and the cost in terms of fuel consumption. During the trip, though, things come up that weren't planned, like having to take a detour or fixing a flat tire. Because of this, the car can't finish the job in the time allotted or for the price expected. It's important to recognize that the car itself is not at fault for these challenges, and instead we should focus on finding ways to adapt and overcome these obstacles. We can't blame the car for not meeting the goals we set for it, nor can we expect it to achieve a certain level of efficiency without taking into account the challenges it faced.

Instead, we should divide our decisions into subsystems. We have a dashboard in the car that tells us if everything is fine with the car and if we need to fix anything or perform maintenance. We also have a GPS navigator to see where we are in relation to our goal. We do not make any decisions about the car relying on a GPS navigator. And we are hardly making any decisions about goals by looking at the dashboard. This is the way to avoid the problem: when we make decisions about payments in appraisals based on some figures, employees start thinking about the figures and not about finding the best way to achieve our goal. You should agree that if your GPS navigator is motivated by showing you some figures, you won't be able to rely on such navigation.

Performance reviews are an important part of any business because they are used to judge how well employees do their jobs and figure out how much they are worth in terms of bonuses and pay. However, traditional performance reviews often focus solely on OKRs (Objectives and Key Results) and fail to take into account the professional characteristics of the employee. This can make people less ambitious because they don't want to set goals that are too hard for fear that they won't be able to reach them, take short cuts, or play the system. There is a good approach to solving this. If we think of employees as characters in a game with unique characteristics like attack, defense, and magic, for example, we can create a more holistic performance review system.

Employees are evaluated based on their professional characteristics rather than whether they met their goals in this game-like approach. Achieving their OKRs is a means of improving these characteristics. Just like in a game where a character must complete missions and defeat beasts and dragons to gain experience and level up, employees must achieve their OKRs to improve their professional characteristics. This way of doing things makes sure that employees not only reach their goals but also learn the skills and abilities they need to do their jobs well. So, to improve the characteristics of their character, employees can achieve their OKRs and do training. This training can come in various forms, such as mentoring, workshops, or on-the-job training. In this way, we have a more fair system of payment and promotion—some kind of meritocracy.

And it will be very beneficial for employees to check how achieving OKRs has improved their professional characteristics, especially if you have personal development plans for employees or a ranking system. Of course, when making plans, it is good when team members are able to see how new goals will fit their characteristics and help them proceed with their personal development plan.

In conclusion, it's important to have separate systems for evaluating employee performance, figuring out pay, and co-ordinating work so that the workplace is fair and encourages people to do their best. Companies can effectively motivate and reward their employees by splitting the incentive system into these three subsystems and managing them separately.

OKR is only about work coordination.

We do not want to know from OKRs:

1. How hard each employee works.
2. What the fair monetary compensation is.
3. Should we move employees to the next stage of the career ladder?

OKR is only used to:

1. Unite us around our common goals.
2. Understand where we are in respect to them.
3. Synchronize between team members and adapt if there are any changes required.

Why do we need regular checkups?

As part of OKR, reconciliations and synchronizations should be done regularly because they are important for making sure the organization is making progress toward its goals and using its resources well. If you look at and measure your progress often and on time, it will be much easier to spot any problems that may come up in the future. As a result, book adjustments may be made as required.

Reconciling and coordinating around our goals on a regular basis helps an organization become more responsive to its members and more open, which makes the organization more effective overall and makes it easier to reach its goals. If clear goals are set and progress toward those goals is evaluated on a regular basis, it is much easier to tell if people or teams are meeting their goals and where more help or resources may be needed. This can be done by setting clear goals and regularly checking to see how well they have been met. So, workers can see how their job fits into the organization's bigger goals, and they may offer comments and suggestions to help make decisions. This might make it simpler for individuals in the organization to communicate with one another and collaborate, which would be beneficial to the organization as a whole.

Regular reconciliations and synchronization also provide workers with the opportunity to keep in touch with the company's objectives and ensure that they are in accordance with those goals by following processes that are in line with those goals. When workers are participating in the process, it is much simpler to build a sense of shared purpose and ensure that everyone is working toward the same objectives as the rest of the organization. This is because it is much simpler to ensure that everyone is working toward the same objectives when everyone is working toward the same goals. Everyone in the organization is working toward the same objective, which might foster a feeling of collaboration and cooperation.

Pay attention to the fact that it is important to make sure that regular synchronizations don't turn into boring reporting and bureaucracy. This will help make sure that they are still useful and effective for the organization. By focusing on clear goals, meeting structure, and agenda, involving employees in the process, and having a good moderator, it is possible to keep the integrity and purpose of the synchronizations and make them a valuable tool for driving progress and success.

Overall, it is important for OKR to do reconciliations and synchronizations often because these activities help make sure that goals are met, promote accountability and transparency, and improve communication and cooperation within the organization. If you make these frequent check-ins a regular part of your company's culture, you will be able to establish a team that works better together, is more successful, and is better able to meet the objectives it has set for itself.

Why do we reduce the number of goals?

I think you should have one to three goals (objectives) per level and three to five key results (metrics) for each goal.

The principle of focus is a crucial aspect of OKR. By reducing the number of goals and focusing on a few key objectives, it becomes easier to measure progress and make necessary adjustments. This is because when we try to control too many things at once, it becomes difficult to measure our progress and make meaningful changes. If we want to reach big goals, we need as few indicators as possible so that we can focus our efforts and make a big step forward in one area.

In addition to making it easier to measure progress and make changes, focusing also helps to create a sense of completion. When we set a single objective and work towards it, we are more likely to feel a sense of accomplishment when we achieve it. This can give us a reason to keep working toward our goals and keep us going.

Furthermore, focus allows us to concentrate everyone's efforts in the same direction. By putting all of our efforts toward the same goal, we can work better together and reach our goals faster. This is why it is important to have just one or a few key goals at each level of the organization, from the company level down to the individual employee level.

And of course, it is impossible to achieve ambitious goals if your attention and resources are dispersed among a huge number of goals and metrics.

Overall, the focus principle is an important part of OKR because it helps us track our progress, make any needed changes, feel like we've accomplished something, and work well together to reach our goals. By focusing our efforts, we can reach more ambitious goals and give everyone in our organization a sense of accomplishment and success.

Principle 30/70

The 30/70 approach in OKR (Objectives and Key Results) is a principle that suggests that 30% of goals should come from the top, such as from senior management or company leaders, while 70% should come from the bottom, such as from employees or teams. This approach is based on the idea that goals are most effective when they are aligned, contain the best engagement, reflect the best strategies, and reflect the best approach.

The 30% of goals that come from the top are typically more strategic in nature and focus on the overall vision and direction of the organization. These goals are often set by senior management or company leaders and are designed to align with the overall mission and objectives of the organization.

On the other hand, the 70% of goals that come from the bottom are more tactical in nature and focus on the day-to-day operations and activities of the organization. These goals are often set by employees or teams and are designed to align with the specific roles and responsibilities of those individuals or teams.

The 30/70 approach is not an exact proportion, but rather a principle stating that fewer goals should come from the top and the majority from the bottom. This approach is designed to ensure that goals are aligned, contain the best engagement, and reflect the best strategies and approaches.

The 30/70 approach allows for a balance of top-down and bottom-up goal-setting. Top-down goals set by senior management provide a clear direction and vision for the organization, while bottom-up goals set by employees and teams provide a more detailed understanding of the day-to-day operations and activities. This balance ensures that the organization is working towards both long-term strategic goals as well as short-term tactical goals.

Furthermore, the 30/70 approach ensures that employees and teams feel more ownership and engagement in achieving their goals. Goals set by employees and teams are more likely to be realistic, achievable, and aligned with their roles and responsibilities. Therefore, they are more likely to be engaged and motivated to achieve these goals.

In conclusion, the 30/70 approach in OKR is a principle that suggests that 30% of goals should come from the top and 70% should come from the bottom. This approach is based on the idea that goals are most effective when they are aligned, contain the best engagement, and reflect the best strategies and approaches. By following this approach, organizations can achieve a balance between top-down and bottom-up goal-setting, ensuring that both long-term strategic goals and short-term tactical goals are met.

How does the implementation of the principles work in practice?

It is impossible to implement all seven principles in a company at once. The transformation usually takes three quarters to complete. It's best to implement them one at a time, never several.

For example, we have a quarter ahead of us. We're going to plan around OKR. Furthermore, we will instill some of the skills and principles in the employees. For example, the principle of regular reconciliation and the principle of focus. All the others will ideally be implemented as well, but later. While planning OKR for this quarter, we are constantly working on measuring and reducing the number of goals and metrics.

In other cases, we set ourselves a task: with OKR formulation this quarter, we are not only moving towards goals but also working on developing the employees' ability to set ambitious goals and monitor their implementation. We then devote this quarter to developing that skill. The fewer skills you take on for a period of time, the more likely you are to develop this habit in people. Don't be too optimistic here. There is no hurry. When we are changing people's mindsets, a slower pace is acceptable.

Basically, each principle listed above is a habit that people need to develop. And skills are hard. For example, when we speak of transparency, not only do we develop the skill of showing everyone our goals, but we also teach them to monitor and control others regularly, helping others to achieve their goals. It's a simple thing, but it takes at least 21 days (actually, an entire quarter) to make it a habit. For example, the skill of setting goals that are ambitious in every sense, thinking "out of the box," and regularly monitoring: "Aren't I trying to achieve my goals using old approaches, or am I looking for new ways? After all, ambitious goals can only be achieved in an ambitious way."

Sometimes, in the early stages of OKR implementation, it is worth agreeing to a partial cascade of goals. For example, the management will prepare all the OKRs themselves and set all the goals for the employees because this quarter we are working on publicity and transparency. So, everyone can see it, come in, look at it, and work with it. Next quarter, we're going to get people involved in goal setting as well. However, each quarter, we only focus on what is important right now.

Or quarterly goals. There's work going on in the format of quarterly goals, but there are employees who are not yet able to think quarterly. They're thinking either a week, a month, or a year. I've met employees who only think in terms of three years. In less than three years, they can't set goals because they're not used to it. This, too, needs to be taught.

To summarize:
1. OKR is first and foremost about habits and ways of thinking.
2. It is important to work on the mindset of our employees to implement OKR correctly and effectively.
3. To do this reliably and firmly, we choose each quarter which of our mindsets we are going to focus on. And then throughout the quarter we pay special attention to developing the skills of this principle in the teams.

How to formulate your OKR correctly

Why it is important to formulate OKR correctly

OKR, which stands for "Objectives and Key Results," is a method for setting goals that many organizations use to set clear, measurable goals and keep track of their progress. However, mistakes in the formulation of OKR can lead to a variety of issues.

One significant issue is that we are losing consistency. When objectives are not properly defined, it can be difficult for an organization to stay on track and maintain a consistent focus on its goals. This can result in a lack of progress and, in the worst-case scenario, failure to meet those objectives.

Another issue is that people forget what is not made clear or reminded of frequently enough. If OKR aren't clearly defined and often reinforced, it's easy for team members to lose sight of their goals and lose motivation. This can result in a lack of progress and accountability for meeting the goals that have been set.

Furthermore, tracking progress is difficult if OKR is not properly formulated. It is impossible to determine whether or not the organization is moving in the right direction and making progress toward its objectives without clear, measurable goals.

Also, if the OKR isn't written correctly, the organization risks not meeting its goals and missing out on opportunities. It's easy to get sidetracked and lose sight of the big picture if you don't have clear, specific goals to strive for. This can lead to missed opportunities and stagnation.

Another problem is that if OKR isn't done right, the organization may start to fall apart. It is easy for team members to work at cross-purposes and pull in different directions when there are no clear, shared goals. This can lead to confusion and stagnation.

Also, if the OKR isn't set up right, routine tasks might get done, but development tasks might be put off. Without a clear focus on the most important tasks and goals, the organization is likely to get off track and fall back on old routines and habits.

Lastly, if OKR is not made correctly, people will be very upset that their time was wasted. Team members can become frustrated and demotivated if there are no clear goals and no clear plan for achieving them. This can result in a lack of productivity and progress.

Mistakes in creating OKRs can lead to a number of problems, such as a lack of consistency, a lack of focus and accountability, missed opportunities, a lack of synchronization, a focus on routine tasks rather than development tasks, and disappointment and frustration among team members. It is critical to ensure that OKRs are properly formulated in order to avoid these issues and ensure the organization's success.

John W. Bergman once said, "There is never enough time to do it right, but there is always enough time to do it over." This quote suggests that it is better to take the time to do things correctly the first time rather than rushing and making mistakes that will require additional time and effort to fix later.

What does OKR consist of?

OKR consists of two main components: objective and key results.

Objectives are the broad, long-term goals that the organization wants to achieve. These goals should be meaningful and inspiring, and they should motivate the organization to strive for excellence. To be effective, goals should be reached within a quarter and be challenging enough to push the organization and make it feel good to be uncomfortable. It's important to only have one main goal at a time, because having too many can make it hard for the organization to stay focused and work hard.

Key results are the specific, measurable goals that an organization must reach to reach its goals. These targets should be clear and easy to understand, and they should be measurable on a weekly basis. Key results may change from week to week as the organization makes progress towards its objectives, and they provide a way for the organization to track its progress and assess whether it is on track to achieve its goals. It is ideal to have three to five key results for each objective, and the sum of all the key results should equal the overall objective. By tracking key results on a regular basis, the organization can identify areas for improvement and make adjustments as needed in order to stay on track and achieve its goals.

Let's see an example.

The objective "Reach self-sufficiency" is a broad, long-term goal that the organization is striving to achieve. Self-sufficiency means being able to take care of your own needs without help from outside sources. This could mean becoming independent in terms of money, food, or energy production, or it could mean becoming independent in terms of manufacturing or production.

To reach this goal, the organization would need to set specific, measurable key results that will help it move toward self-sufficiency. Some possible key results for this objective could include:

1. Increase revenue by X% in the next quarter.
2. Achieve X% reduction in reliance on external suppliers.
3. Increase production efficiency by X% in the next quarter.
4. Develop and implement a plan to become energy self-sufficient.

By setting key results like these, the organization can track its progress toward self-sufficiency and make changes as needed to make sure it is on track to reach its goal.

OKR models and strategies

Now we are going to talk about the three types of OKR models:
1. How we can cascade OKRs through the company.
2. How we can set OKRs in terms of time periods.
3. Strategies for formulating OKR.

How we can cascade OKRs through the company.

There are three strategies to cascade OKRs through the company:

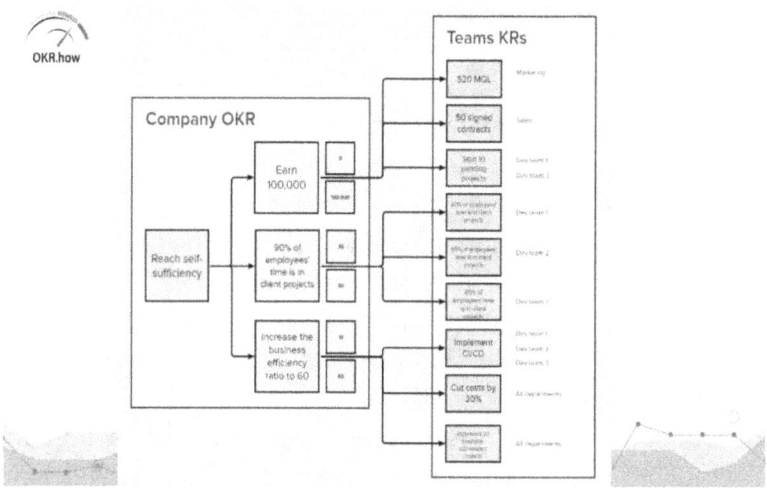

The first strategy involves having a structure with company-level goals and key results and then breaking down key results into indicators at the team level. In this model, teams do not have common goals; only key results are linked to company-level key results. This model is flexible, gives the fastest results, saves money, and is easy to recalculate and sync, but it may not have as much of an effect on the organization's corporate culture. Usually, we start implementing OKR with this strategy.

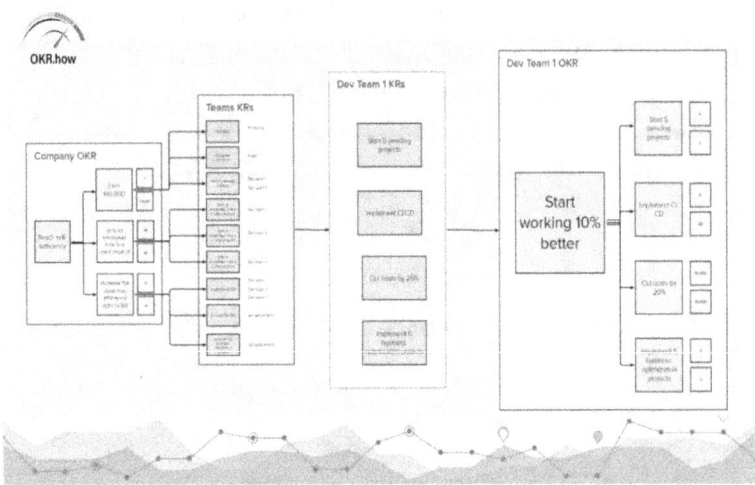

The second strategy involves having company-level goals and key results, and then each department has its own set of goals and key results that are linked to the company-level key results. So we start the same way with the first strategy. After we've formulated company-level OKR and broken it down into team-level indicators, we transform those indicators into teams' OKR. This model takes more time to make, but it may have a bigger effect on the culture of the company because employees are involved in setting their own goals in the OKR way. Some companies adopted this strategy after the third quarter of OKR implementation.

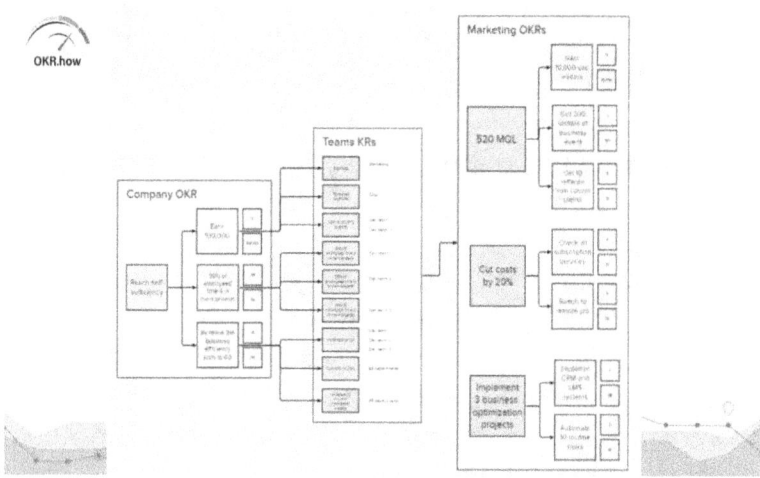

The third strategy involves having company-level goals and key results, with each key result becoming an objective for a different department. The department establishes key results for their objectives. The department's key results become the employees' goals, and the employees set their own key results based on their goals. This model makes the most sense and might have the biggest effect on the culture of the company, but it might also take the longest to put into place. It takes a lot of coordination and communication between departments and employees to make sure that everyone is working toward the same goals and helping the organization reach its goals as a whole. It also has a very high chance of getting off track because it has so many goals and key results. When we look at the final tree of goals in this strategy, it is the least succinct. Only a few companies have used that model for a long time, though a lot starts with it if a company is implementing the OKR approach by itself without an OKR coach.

How we can set OKRs in terms of time periods.

Based on time, there are three main ways to set OKR: planning once a year, planning every three months, and planning every six months.

The first strategy involves setting goals for the entire year and then breaking them down into goals for each division. This model is easy to formulate as it is familiar and clear, and it saves time during the planning process. However, it may not be adaptable to changes that may occur throughout the year. This model works well for businesses that operate in markets that are fairly stable and predictable, where there aren't many big changes in the industry or business. We use this strategy very rarely while implementing OKRs in companies.

The second strategy involves setting a yearly goal as a beacon and then setting quarterly goals, but only for the first quarter for the company and each division. This model allows for flexibility as it allows for adjustments to be made on a quarterly basis. But it takes more time to plan because you have to set both yearly and quarterly goals. This model is good for businesses that work in markets that are more dynamic and unpredictable, where the industry or business may go through big changes. This is the most widely used OKR model as it gives a lot of benefits and is not too time- or resource-consuming.

In terms of planning time and adaptability, the third strategy falls somewhere in the middle of the first two. It involves setting a six-month goal for the company and breaking it down into six-month goals for each division. This model gives you a little bit of flexibility and takes less time to plan than the quarterly model. Companies in the real economy and companies that can't afford quarterly strategic planning sessions usually use this model.

It is important to think about the planning horizon when choosing a strategy for making OKR. The planning horizon is the length of time over which the organization and the person are able to plan their activities. If the planning horizon is too short, the organization might not have enough time to carry out its plans well. On the other hand, if the planning horizon is too long, the organization may not be able to adapt to changes that occur in the market or industry. During the planning process, it is important to find the right balance between being flexible and having a plan for the long term.

Strategies for formulating OKR.

There are different ways to come up with goals and key results, and each has its own pros and cons.

The first strategy is "From Objectives to Key Results."

Start with a vision or goal for the company, and then create key results to track progress toward that goal. It is important that the goal be motivating, inspiring, and comprehensive. The company then develops a set of key results to track progress toward the goal. These key outcomes must be specific and measurable. Key results could include increasing revenue, lowering expenses, or entering new markets. While this is the best approach, it may not always be possible to use it in all situations because not all businesses can begin with a goal or vision. This approach, however, is generally the best and should be used whenever possible.

The second strategy is "From Key Results to Objectives."

Companies with a lot of inertia often use an approach to setting goals that involves finding existing indicators or metrics and using them to set the goal.

Some of these metrics, like sales and the number of stores, may have been set up in the past and are hard to change. To use this approach, the company looks at the indicators and determines the goal based on them.

For example, let's say the company has the following revenue and turnover set as indicators for the current period:

Revenue: $500,000
Turnover: $1,000,000

Based on these figures, the company can determine that it is an experienced exporter.

Once the goal is set (in our example, "to become an experienced exporter"), the company can look at the key indicators to see if they are enough to reach the goal. If not, any missing key results can be added. The company can then check to make sure the sum of the key results equals the goal and make any necessary adjustments.

For example, after a few rounds of checks, we can finish with such an OKR:

Objective: To become an experienced exporter
Key Results:
    1. Achieve a revenue of $500,000

2. Achieve a turnover of $1,000,000
3. Increase exports to at least 50 countries
4. Establish partnerships with at least 5 well-known international clients
5. Obtain at least 3 industry certifications.

This approach is not always the best, but it can be useful in certain situations.

The third strategy is "From Tasks and initiatives to Key Results and then to Objective."

We might use a third way to come up with goals and key results in certain situations. If we can't use indicators or metrics to figure out the goal, this method starts with making a list of tasks that need to be done. This approach is often used in service departments where the goal may be more fluid or subject to change. To use this method, we first figure out what needs to be done, like opening an office in a certain place or making a start in a certain market. We then group these tasks into sectors and determine what key result we want to achieve in each sector. Using this approach, we can turn our set of tasks into key results and then use them to create an overall goal, using the same algorithms as in the second strategy. This approach can be useful when it is very difficult to start with the formulation of objectives or key results.

For example, a company may have a goal to expand its services into a new region. The owner of the business may give the service department specific tasks, such as opening an office in the new area, hiring local workers, and forming partnerships with other local businesses. The service department can then look at these tasks and determine what key results it needs to achieve in order to meet the overall goal of expansion. For example, they might set key results like the number of new clients they get, the share of the market in the new area, and the amount of money they make from the new area. Once these key results are set, the company can use these metrics to track its progress toward its growth goal.

So, we start with tasks, then combine them into Key Results and then continue to formulate OKR using the approach "From Key Results to Objective".

In conclusion, there are various strategies for cascading and setting OKRs within a company. The first strategy involves having company-level goals and key results and breaking down key results into indicators at the team level. The right strategy for a company will depend on things like the industry it works in, how flexible it needs to be, and what effect it wants to have on its corporate culture.

Steps for correct OKR planning

The process of formulating OKRs begins with setting a big, ambitious goal for the company (BHAG). Some companies then prepare an annual roadmap to that goal. Regardless of whether you make a plan to achieve a big, ambitious goal broken down by year or not, the next thing we need is this OKR for the coming year. Next, the company makes a plan every three months for how to reach this annual goal. The quarterly goal is transformed into an OKR. It is more specific and is not expected to change during the quarter. However, the roadmap for the annual goal may be periodically reviewed. Each team within the company then determines what they will do to contribute to the achievement of the quarterly company goals. This includes setting specific outcomes that they will work toward. Finally, the teams coordinate with each other to ensure that everyone is on track to meet their commitments and contribute to the overall goal of the company. And we end up having:

1. BHAG;
2. Goal for the current year;
3. Quarterly roadmap to annual goal;
4. Company OKR for the nearest quarter;
5. Based on contribution to the company goal and help to other departments - OKR for each team.

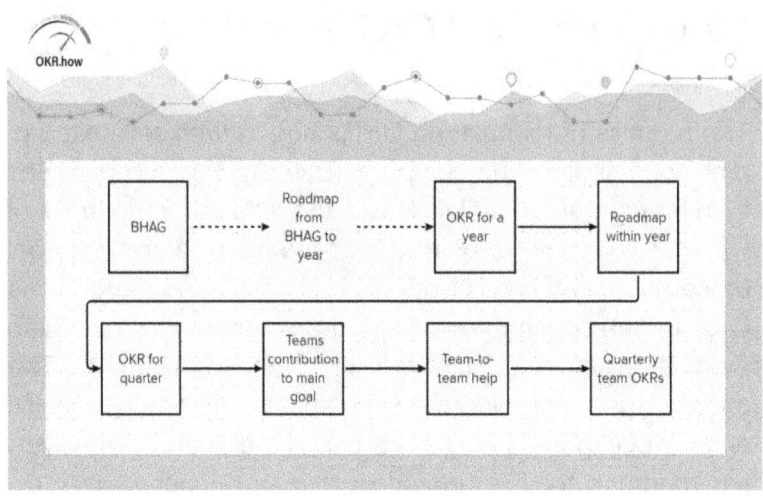

For example, a company may have a BHAG of becoming the leading provider of a certain product in their industry. They might make an annual plan to reach this goal that includes things like expanding their network of distributors, putting out new products, and doing more marketing. The company then sets an OKR for the current year of increasing their market share by 20%. To reach this annual goal, the company makes a quarterly plan with specific steps like launching a new product in Q1, putting more effort into marketing in Q2, and expanding the distribution network in Q3. The company's OKR for Q1 may be to launch the new product and achieve a 10% increase in sales. Then, each team in the company, like the product development team and the marketing team, will come up with its own OKRs that help the company reach its Q1 goal. The OKR for the product development team could be to finish making the new product on time. The OKR for the marketing team could be to start a successful marketing campaign for the new product. Finally, the teams will coordinate with each other to ensure that everyone is meeting their commitments and working towards the overall goal of the company.

If we've followed the OKR approach correctly, we should have four strategic planning sessions per year: one large annual meeting and three smaller quarterly meetings.

Checklist what is important to prepare in advance before formulating OKR for your team.

There are a few key inputs that you will need to receive from the company in order to formulate your team's OKRs:

- ✓ The company's BHAG (Big Hairy Ambitious Goal) - This is the overall goal that the company is working towards and will provide the context for your team's OKRs.
- ✓ The company's annual goals - These are the intermediate goals that the company is working towards in order to achieve the BHAG. Understanding these goals will help you align your team's OKRs with the overall direction of the company.
- ✓ The company's quarterly roadmap - This will provide you with an idea of what the company is focusing on in the current quarter and can help you prioritize your team's OKRs accordingly.
- ✓ Any relevant company-level OKRs - If there are any company-level OKRs that are relevant to your team, you will need to be aware of them in order to ensure that your team's OKRs are aligned with them.
- ✓ Top managers' input: Your top manager will have ideas and goals for your team that should be taken into account when making OKR. Make sure to communicate with them and gather their input.
- ✓ Input from other teams: Your team's OKR may be interconnected with the OKR of other teams. It is important to understand their goals and how your team can support or depend on them.
- ✓ Team's capabilities and resources: Consider the skills, knowledge, and resources of your team when

formulating OKR. Make sure the goals are challenging, but also realistic and achievable given the team's current capabilities.
- ✓ Feedback from team members - In order to formulate effective OKRs for your team, it is important to gather input and feedback from team members about their priorities and goals. This will help you ensure that the OKRs you set are meaningful and relevant to your team.

How to formulate a goal/objective

First of all, you should reconsider your attitude toward targets.

The goal is not something that we think up "for the tick" so that there is something to wish for in the New Year. It is a chance to give 100%, to test your limits, and to give of yourself. If you use this scale to evaluate your goals, you will slowly become someone for whom anything is possible.

When formulating an objective in an OKR, there are four main options to consider:

1. **Reaching a new level**: This involves setting a goal to achieve a new level of success or growth in the company or a specific product. For example, "Increase company revenue by 20% over the next year."

2. **Doing something in a new way**: This involves setting a goal to approach a task or process in a new and innovative way. For example, "Implement a new customer service strategy that improves customer satisfaction by 50% within six months."

3. **A cardinal increase in a specific metric:** This means setting a goal to get a big jump in a certain metric. For example, "Increase website traffic by 50% within the next quarter."

4. **Creation of something new**: This involves setting a goal to create something that does not currently

exist within the company. For example, "Develop and launch a new product line within the next year."

When formulating a goal in OKR, it is important to consider the following points:

1. **Look into the eyes:** The goal should inspire and motivate employees to work towards it. It should be something that resonates with them and makes them feel like they are part of something bigger.

2. **Clear and catchy:** The goal should be clear and easy to understand, but it does not have to be formulated in a specific way. It can be catchy and memorable, as long as it effectively communicates what needs to be achieved.

3. **Align with employee benefits:** The language used in the goal should be consistent with the benefits that employees will receive from achieving it. For example, if the goal is to increase revenue, it is fair to assume that employees will be motivated by the potential for increased bonuses or commissions. If you want to use non-monetary motivation, the objective should not be about money.

4. **Be honest:** It is important to be honest and realistic when formulating a goal. Do not try to write a goal about becoming the best company in the world if you are not actively working towards that goal. Focus on what can realistically be achieved and be transparent with employees about what they can expect.

Let's discuss some examples of Objectives.

Winter is coming. (Get prepared for a low season.)

In an effort to motivate their team and prepare for a slow season, a company used the phrase "Winter is coming" as an objective in their OKR. This phrase, inspired by a popular TV show, resonated with the team because they all enjoyed the show and were able to easily understand the objective. It motivated them to come up with creative ways to improve their performance during the slow season. By using language that was meaningful to the team and tapping into their shared interests, the company was able to set a clear and inspiring goal that helped boost morale and drive results. This way of making OKR goals shows how important it is to think about the interests and motivations of the team in order to make goals that are both effective and interesting.

Establish a $1,000,000 cancer foundation.

The company in the next example was solely focused on making money and did not have any other priorities or values. When it came time to set an objective in their OKR, the team had to be honest and realistic about their priorities. They knew that any goals they set that were not directly related to making money would not be taken seriously. Therefore, they focused on setting financial targets. However, they also recognized the importance of having a purpose behind those targets. They asked themselves why they were setting a specific financial goal and looked for a deeper meaning behind it. In one case, the team members' own experiences with cancer led them to decide to try to raise $1 billion to fight the disease. This gave the financial goals a sense of purpose and helped to motivate the team. In other cases, the team did not have any specific causes or values that they wanted to align their goals with and instead focused solely on the financial targets.

Provide employees with salaries above the market

It is important for a company to be honest about its goals and to consider the reasoning behind the objectives it sets, especially if those objectives involve making a certain amount of money. In one case, a company set a goal to provide salaries above the market to their employees. In another case, the company wanted to use their profits to make a positive impact on society by restoring a factory, stadium, or bridge in a war-torn region. It is crucial to think about the meaning behind the monetary goals that a company sets, rather than just focusing on the money itself. This can help make sure the goals are inspiring and serve a purpose other than just making more money. So if you need to formulate a goal about money, ask yourself and your team why we need this amount of money.

Create an infinitely scalable platform using asynchronous Python code

In the third example, a division of the company used a unique and unconventional goal in their OKR. While other goals such as "becoming the best in the market" or "becoming like SpaceX in our industry" did not motivate the team, this goal sparked excitement and enthusiasm. Even though it didn't follow the usual rules for setting goals, it did a good job of motivating employees and aligning with key results. The main thing to remember is that the goal should have meaning, have steps that can be taken, and be attainable. It's important not to get too caught up in a specific formula for goal formulation but rather focus on creating a goal that motivates and inspires the team.

Become a sex symbol for employees

In today's competitive job market, it's important for a company's success to find and keep top talent. One company recognized this and decided to take a unique approach to the problem by setting a goal to become a "sex symbol" for their employees. This goal may seem unconventional, but it helped the company think creatively about ways to make their workplace more desirable and attractive to employees. By focusing on becoming a "sex symbol," the company was able to come up with innovative strategies to improve employee satisfaction and retention. This unconventional goal ultimately helped the company solve their problem of not having enough people and contributed to their overall success. While this approach may not work for every company, it shows the importance of setting meaningful goals that can inspire and motivate employees to take action.

Switch from sticks to shovels

The company wanted to improve their performance and decided to set a goal of updating their outdated tools and technology. They recognized that they were using old and inferior tools compared to their competitors. The metaphor that emerged during brainstorming was as if they were prehistoric people digging holes with digging sticks while everybody around them was using excavators. So, they wanted to at least catch up to using basic, modern tools like shovels. They made it clear what their current situation was by using old tools, like digging with sticks, and what they wanted their future situation to be by using modern tools, like shovels.

This goal was important because it solved a specific problem the company was having and showed how to make things better.

It can be beneficial for a company to have two objectives: one for the company itself and another for their product. This allows the company to focus on both internal operations and the external impact it is trying to have. It is important not to have too many goals, as this can become overwhelming and hinder progress. Instead, it is best to focus on a few key objectives that align with the overall mission of the company. It is also important to remember that each department and individual team should have their own goals rather than trying to set goals for every department or individual at the company level. By setting goals at the right level, you can have a clear and focused plan for how to reach your goals.

When setting goals, it is important not to confuse cause and effect. It is not productive to start by considering the resources available, such as the number of people or amount of money, and then formulate goals based on those resources. Instead, it is more effective to start by defining the desired outcome and then think about what resources are needed to achieve that outcome. After figuring out what resources are needed, it's important to figure out what's already there and what needs to be added or taken away in order to reach the goal. This approach ensures that the focus is on the desired outcome rather than the constraints of the resources. It also avoids setting goals based on what is already available rather than what is truly desired.

Here are some bad examples of objectives in OKR:

1. Improve your work -> this is not the goal; this is routing without a clear ending.
2. Boost performance -> this goal is too vague and doesn't have a clear end.
3. Improve the development process -> the same problem as with previous.
4. Beat the geese, bring the money -> it's not clear what it's about.
5. Earn 15% more -> hardly anyone will feel involved, but this can be considered as a good Key Result.

Overall, it's important to set clear and involving goals that provide context and direction, and to understand the reasons behind the goals you set.

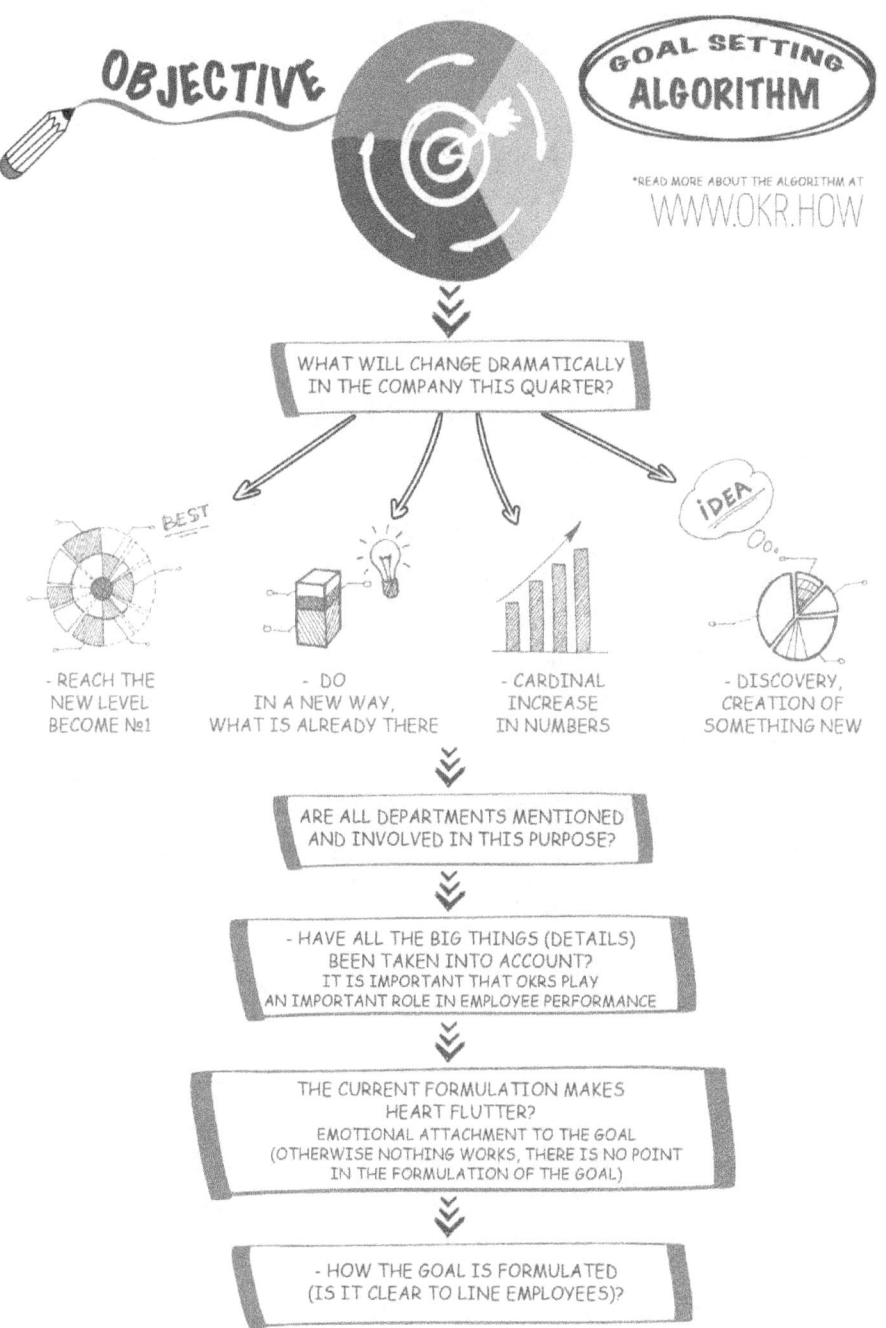

How to formulate Key Results

Let's move on to discussing key results. As we've already said, key results help us see if we are meeting our goals and making progress toward our desired outcomes. Now, let's focus on how to effectively formulate key results.

Key Results are coordinates.

There are two types of metrics: acceptance criteria and coordinates. Acceptance criteria are used to determine whether or not a goal has been reached, but they are often not useful in the process of working towards the goal because they are usually binary ("yes or no"). Coordinates, on the other hand, are a more universal system of notation that can be used to measure progress towards a goal and determine if adaptations need to be made. When setting key results, it is important to use coordinates instead of acceptance criteria because key results are a way to keep track of progress and make sure everyone is working at the same time. Acceptance criteria can be helpful when looking back at what happened, but they are not helpful when working toward a goal.

Here are some more examples of acceptance criteria and coordinates:

Acceptance criteria:
1. A software program has zero bugs.
2. A student receives an A grade on an exam.
3. A new product launch is successful.

Coordinates:
1. The number of bugs in the software program decreases by 25% each month.
2. The student's exam scores improve by 10% each semester.
3. The number of products sold in the first month increases by at least 50% compared to the previous product launch.

Again, acceptance criteria are the specific conditions that must be met for a goal to be considered accomplished, while coordinates are ways to measure how close you are to the goal.

Five approaches for formulation of Key Results.

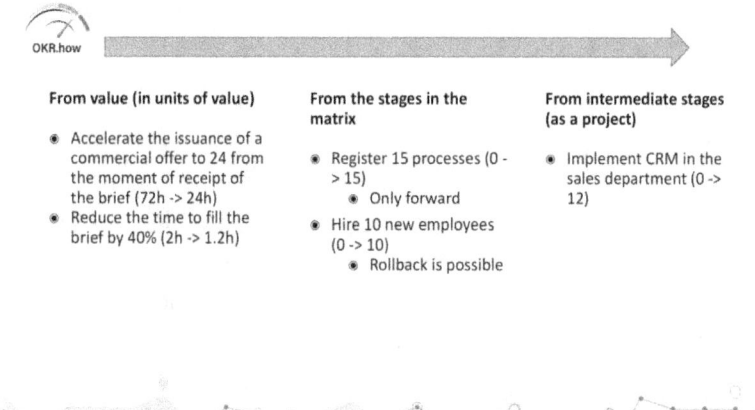

There are five ways to come up with key results. The first three are the best, and the last two should only be used if the first three don't work. The first option is the best, and it is recommended that you try to use this option first. If it is not possible, then the second and third options should be tried. If none of these options work, the fourth and fifth options can be used. It is important to try to use the best options whenever possible.

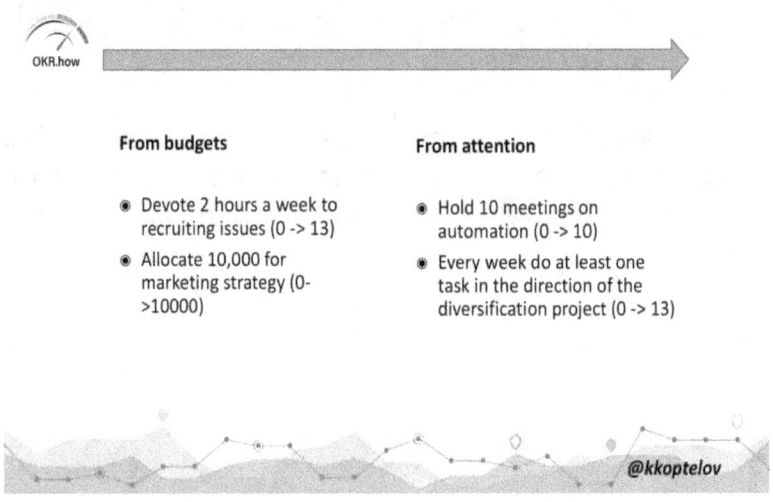

Measuring the value

One option for tracking progress towards a goal is to use units of value, such as dollars, hours, or the amount of a particular resource gained or lost. Value-based metrics are a powerful tool for monitoring development and accomplishing outcomes. Measuring value lets us evaluate the real benefits and results of our work, instead of just keeping track of the steps we take to reach a goal. This might help you learn what is working and what you may need to change to be more successful.

Let's use the goal of improving company efficiency as an illustration. Time saved as a result of streamlining a process could be used as a metric towards this end. If we keep an eye on this statistic, we can see the results of our work and know if we're making headway. Time savings that grow over time may be an indication that our efforts are successful and that we are making progress. On the other hand, if we see that the amount of time saved stays the same or goes down, it may be time to rethink our approach and make changes that will help us reach our goal more quickly.

Value-based metrics for tracking development help keep our attention on the objective. To figure out the best ways to measure our progress, we need to think about what we want to accomplish and why it's important. If we want to increase our earnings, tracking the amount of money made from the sale of a specific product may be a better indicator of success than counting the number of times that product has been purchased.

When evaluating success, we can use a wide variety of metrics, not just the amount of time or money saved or earned. Rates of consumer satisfaction, market share, and employee retention might all be monitored. By keeping an eye on these indicators, we can see how customers and staff react to our efforts, which lets us make changes as needed.

Overall, it is more thorough and effective to measure development in terms of value. It is possible to see the results of our efforts and make educated choices about how to improve by keeping tabs on key metrics on a regular basis. Staying focused and on track while making sure our efforts are having the desired effect requires paying attention to what is truly important and what is propelling our progress.

Using leading indicators for important results is a smart idea because they show real-time progress towards targets. Leading indicators change before the final result, therefore they can anticipate future performance. By monitoring leading indicators, we can tell if we're on pace to reach our goals and make modifications as needed. This helps us keep focused and ensures we're making progress.

Depending on the purpose and industry, many leading indicators might be used. A company that wants to make its customers happier may keep track of how long it takes to respond to customer questions or good feedback. Customer satisfaction levels can change later than leading indicators. By keeping track of these measures on a regular basis, the company can see how far it has come in improving customer satisfaction and make any changes it needs to stay on track.

A company improving employee engagement is another example. Leading indicators may include staff participation in company activities or professional development opportunities. By measuring these things, the company can see if it's making progress toward getting employees more involved and make any necessary changes.

When we use leading indicators for important results, we can track our progress toward our goals in real time and make changes as needed. By monitoring leading indicators, we can stay focused and verify that we're making progress.

Progress may not always be able to be measured in terms of value because of physical limitations or company rules. For example, a company might not want all of its employees to know about its sales or profits. Or the thing we want to measure is behind. One example is the employee net promoter score (eNPC). This metric can be a good way to tell how healthy and successful a business is, since employees who are engaged and happy are more likely to be productive and dedicated to the company's goals. But if eNPC is only measured every six months or once a year, it might not give a clear picture of how engaged employees are right now. In these situations, you may need to think of other ways to track progress, like using a matrix to measure intermediate states or keeping track of the steps you take to reach your goal.

Measuring intermediate states using matrix

One way to track progress in OKR (Objectives and Key Results) is through the use of a matrix or table. This can be especially useful for Key Results where we need to perform the same actions on different objects. It allows for a clear understanding of where the project stands at any given time.

Imagine that a company is working on adding three new features to a software product they already have. These features might be called "Feature A," "Feature B," and "Feature C." In order to make these features, there may be several steps in between, like researching requirements, designing solutions, coding, testing, and writing documentation.

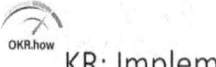

KR: Implement two sprints (Release some specific product functionality)

	Research	Preparing outline	In progress	Testing	Tech Docs	User Guides
Client's personal account on the website (feature 1)						
Analytics of system usage (feature 2)						
New menu option (feature 3)						

Starting point – 0   Finish point – 6*3=18

To track progress, the company could create a matrix or table with the names of the features in the rows and the intermediate steps in the columns. For each key result, the team could track the progress of each feature by marking the corresponding cell with a certain color or symbol. For example, a green cell might indicate that the key result has been completed, while a red cell might indicate that the key result is behind schedule.

By tracking progress in this way, the company can get a clear understanding of where each feature stands at any given time. If a key result takes longer than expected, the team can figure out what's going on and fix it to get the feature back on track. Also, by putting this information in a clear visual format, the company can easily tell stakeholders what is going on with the project and keep them up to date on the progress.

Another example might be a key result of hiring new employees. The recruitment process might involve intermediate steps such as posting job openings, reviewing resumes, conducting interviews, and making offers to candidates. The company could use a matrix with the names of the open positions in the rows and the intermediate steps in the columns. By tracking these vacancies in a matrix or table, it is easier to see how far along the company is in the hiring process and to identify any issues that need to be addressed.

 KR: Find all needed staff for XXX team

	Vacancy posted	Response received	There is a candidate with the first interview	There is a candidate with a second interview	Job Offer Sent	Job Offer Accepted	First working day
PHP Developer							
Tester							
Tech Writer							

* Rollback possible
(OKR is not a reporting system, but a synchronization system)

Here we should talk about the "rollbacks." In the context of the hiring process, a "rollback" means that you have to go back to an earlier stage to find a new candidate for a job. This might occur if the top candidate for a position declines the offer or falls out of the race for any other reason.

For instance, consider a company that has an open position for a courier. They posted the job, looked at the resumes, held interviews, and chose the best person for the job. However, this candidate declines the offer, and the position is once again open. In this situation, the company would need to go back to earlier stages of the recruitment process in order to find a new candidate. This could mean looking at resumes that were turned down before or having more interviews with candidates who were turned down before.

By keeping track of progress in a matrix or table, the company can see where setbacks have happened and take steps to fix them. It also helps to keep the focus on the goal of filling open positions rather than on the amount of work that has been done. This helps to keep the focus on results and allows for more effective communication and adaptation as the process moves forward.

Rollbacks can be painful because it is difficult to see yourself regress on a task for which you have worked hard. But let me remind you that OKR is a system to understand where we are with respect to our goals, not to track how hard we are working.

Tracking as a project.

The third way to track progress toward a goal in OKR (Objectives and Key Results) is to use steps or milestones, like in a project, to measure progress.

This means breaking down a goal into smaller, more manageable steps and tracking progress through those steps. For example, if the goal is to implement a new system, the steps in between might be to make a plan, get approvals, and put the plan into action.

It is important to try to make the intermediate steps roughly equal in size and to have as many steps as possible (ideally more than 13). This helps to better understand and track progress towards the overall goal. It is also helpful to consider the specific actions or tasks that need to be completed in each step in order to better understand and measure progress. This method can be especially helpful when a goal is complicated or has many parts because it makes it easier to track progress in more detail.

In this approach, measuring progress towards a key result (KR) in steps rather than as a percentage from 0% to 100% can be more effective because it allows for a clearer understanding of what is being tracked and how progress is being made.

Expressing key results as percentages can lead to subjective assessments and inaccurate progress reports. This is because it can be difficult to understand what each percentage represents, especially when the key result has not been broken down into specific stages or steps. For example, if you are asked about progress on a key result and you estimate that you are at 5%, your assessment may be based on your feelings rather than on concrete, measurable actions. Also, if you are asked about your progress again in the future and say you are at 10%, it may be hard to compare the two estimates because you are using your memory and feelings instead of specific, measurable actions. It is usually easier to track progress and find problems if key results are broken down into specific stages or steps.

Most of the time, it's best to break up big goals into smaller steps that take less than a week to complete. This can make it easier to keep track of progress and spot any problems that might come up. For example, let's say you are working on a project to design and launch a new website for your company. The key result you are trying to achieve is launching the new website by a certain date. Instead of expressing

this key result as a percentage, you could break it down into specific stages or steps, such as:
1. Define the project scope and objectives.
2. Conduct user research to gather requirements and preferences.
3. Create a content plan and outline.
4. Design the overall layout and user flow of the website.
5. Design wireframes for individual pages and features
6. Create visual mockups for the website.
7. Develop a project plan and timeline.
8. Set up a testing and development environment.
9. Write and implement code for the website.
10. Test the website and fix any issues or bugs.
11. Conduct user testing and gather feedback.
12. Make any final changes or updates to the website.
13. Launch the website.

So, we have Key Results: "launch a new website for your company." starting point: 0; target: 13

By breaking down the key result into smaller steps, you can keep better track of progress and spot any problems that might arise. Also, breaking the main goal into smaller steps can make the project easier to handle and improve its chances of success. In this example, each step is about 5% of the total work done toward the main goal, which is launching the website. This allows for more frequent check-ins and the ability to adjust the plan as needed if something changes between check-ins. Let me know if you have any questions or if you would like further clarification.

Measuring budgets.

One other way to measure key results is through budgets. For example, if a company has a goal of hiring more employees, the director may allocate a certain amount of time each week to review resumes and conduct interviews. This budget of time can be tracked to see if the goal of hiring more employees is being met. Another way to measure key results through budgets is to allocate a certain amount of money for a specific task, such as a marketing campaign. The task of the marketing team would then be to effectively use that budget to reach their goals.

It's important to note that measuring key results through budgets requires clear guidelines on what it means to "use the budget effectively." This could include specific metrics like the number of leads or the marketing campaign's return on investment. It's also important to track progress regularly to ensure that the budget is being used in the most effective way possible. By using budgets to track key results, companies can make sure they are using their resources in the best way possible to reach their goals.

Here are some additional examples of when measuring key results through budgets might be useful:

1. A company has a goal of increasing website traffic, but they are not sure of the best way to do it. They allocate a budget for the marketing team to use for search engine optimization, social media advertising, and other tactics to increase website traffic. They track their progress towards the goal through the budget that has been allocated for these efforts.

2. A company has a goal of launching a new product, but they are not sure of the best way to market it. They allocate a budget for the marketing team to use for market research, advertising, and other tactics to promote the product. They track their progress towards the goal through the budget that has been allocated for these efforts.

3. A company has a goal of improving customer satisfaction, but they are not sure of the best way to do it. They allocate a budget for the customer service team to use for training, new tools and technology, and other efforts to improve the customer experience. They track their progress towards the goal through the budget that has been allocated for these efforts.

4. A company has a goal of expanding into a new market, but they are not sure of the best way to do it. They allocate a budget for the business development team to use for market research, partnerships, and other efforts to enter the new market. They track their progress towards the goal through the budget that has been allocated for these efforts.

In conclusion, measuring key results through budgets is a useful tool for tracking progress towards specific goals, especially when a company is not sure of the best course of action to take or has limited resources.

Tracking attention.

The last way to measure key results is through attention or focusing on a specific task or area of development. This can be useful in situations where there is a high level of uncertainty, and it is not clear how much budget or resources should be allocated to a specific task.

For example, a company may have a goal of automating a specific process, but they are not sure of the best way to do it or how much budget to allocate. In this case, they may set a goal of having at least 10 meetings on automation and track their progress towards the goal through the number of meetings that are held. Another example might be a company that has the goal of diversifying its product line but is not sure of the best way to do it. They may set a goal of doing at least one task every week in the direction of diversification and track their progress through the number of tasks that are completed.

Measuring key results through attention is also helpful when the goal is to help employees or you develop a certain skill or habit. For example, a company may have a goal of improving customer service and may set a goal for customer service team members to have at least 10 interactions with customers every week. By tracking their progress through the number of interactions that are held, the company can help employees develop the habit of consistently providing high levels of customer service.

Another example might be a company that is working to establish a new corporate culture. They may set a goal of having at least three team-building activities every month and track their progress through the number of activities that are held. This can help to build a culture of teamwork and collaboration within the company.

Measuring key results through attention can also be useful in situations where a company is working to transform its business model or operations. For example, a company may want to switch to a more sustainable business model and may decide to do at least three environmentally friendly things every month. By tracking their progress through the number of practices that are implemented, the company can work towards their goal of becoming more sustainable.

It's important to note that measuring key results through attention can be an imprecise method as it relies on subjective measures of progress. However, it can be helpful when there is a lot of uncertainty and other ways of measuring are not possible. By focusing on specific tasks or areas of development and tracking progress regularly, companies can work towards their goals even in the face of uncertainty.

Use MECE when it is possible while formulating KRs.

The MECE (Mutually Exclusive, Collectively Exhaustive) principle is a way of organizing and dividing information into distinct, non-overlapping categories. It is used a lot in business, especially when figuring out what the key results (KRs) are for OKRs (Objectives and Key Results).

The MECE principle consists of three components: mutually exclusive, collectively exhaustive, and equal size.

Mutually exclusive means that the categories should not overlap or have any common elements. For example, you might divide the KRs for a marketing campaign into two groups: online marketing efforts and offline marketing efforts. These categories should be distinct from one another, so that no KR falls into more than one category.

Collectively exhaustive means that all of a set's parts should be covered by the categories. In the example above, if we define our KR categories as online marketing efforts and offline marketing efforts, then every KR related to the marketing campaign should fit into one of these categories.

Equal size means that the workload or length of time for each category should be about the same. For example, if you are defining KRs for a quarter, you might have an equal number of KRs in each category, or you might have KRs that are of similar size and scope within each category.

In short, the MECE principle is a good way to organize and divide KRs into different groups that don't overlap, cover everything, and are the same size. It can help make sure that everything that needs to be done is done and that each KR is a manageable size. This makes it easier to track progress and measure success.

ORDER IN CHAOS by Kostiantyn Koptelov

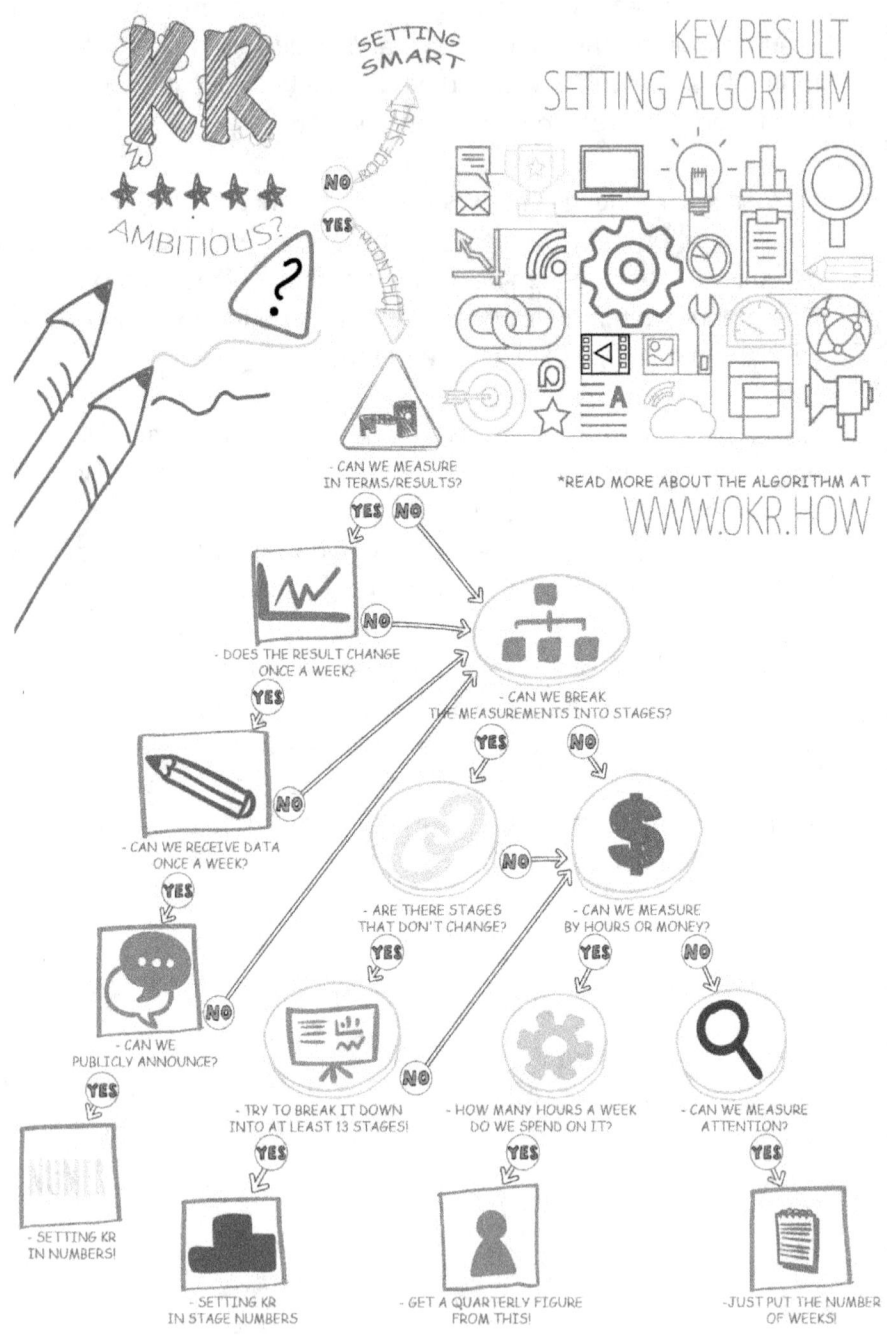

Checklist for formulating a good Key Result.

When you have formulated your key results, check them against this checklist:

- ✓ Can the key result be publicly stated and internally communicated?
- ✓ Do you know where to get the necessary data to measure the key result?
- ✓ Is it possible for the key result to change on a weekly basis?
- ✓ Does the key result contribute towards achieving the overall goal?
- ✓ Are the key results not sequential, with one leading to the next?
- ✓ Is the key result measurable, with a clear way to track progress and determine success?
- ✓ Can the key result be measured on a weekly basis?
- ✓ Does the key result align with the overall strategy, mission and values of the company?
- ✓ Is the key result relevant and important to the team or individual responsible for achieving it?
- ✓ Does the key result have a clear connection to the overall goal, and contribute towards its achievement?
- ✓ Does the Sum of KRs equal to objective?
- ✓ Is the key result realistic, taking into account the team's capacity and other constraints?
- ✓ Does the key result allow for flexibility and adaptability in the case of unexpected changes or challenges?

Examples of OKRs

Below, you will see examples of Objectives and key results. Remember, if you see a key result that seems binary (i.e., either achieved or not achieved), there are likely intermediate steps or projects that contribute to the overall achievement of that key result. It is important to break down large goals into smaller, measurable steps to track progress and ensure success.

Please keep in mind that the OKR examples provided below are for illustration purposes only and should not be used as-is for your company. It is important to make sure that your OKRs fit the needs of your company by taking into account its current stage of development, resources, staff, corporate culture, values, market, and other factors. If you just copy and paste these examples without thinking about how they apply to your company, that won't help. Use these examples to help you come up with your own OKRs that match the goals and objectives of your company.

IT outsourcing company.

Objective: **Create a world-class customer experience.**
Key Results:
1. Implement a customer feedback system and act on 80% of customer feedback.
2. Train all customer-facing employees on best practices and track improvement.
3. Develop and launch a customer rewards program.
4. Roll out a new, easy-to-use customer portal.
5. Respond to all customer inquiries within 1 hour during business hours.

Objective: **Expand our service offerings into new markets.**
Key Results:
1. Research and identify c 3 potential new markets.
2. Develop and launch 1 new service offering for each new market.
3. Secure 5 pilot customers in each new market.
4. Achieve a 50% customer retention rate in each new market.
5. Achieve a profit margin of 20% in each new market.

Software development company.

Objective: Become the leading provider of XYZ software in our industry.
Key Results:
1. Increase our market share by 10.
2. Launch a new version of our software with c 3 major new features.
3. Increase customer retention by 20% through the implementation of a new customer success program.
4. Attend c 2 industry conferences and present on a panel or as a keynote speaker.
5. Achieve a Net Promoter Score of 10.

Objective: Foster a culture of innovation and continuous learning.
Key Results:
1. Implement a new idea management system and achieve c 50 submissions per month.
2. Launch a new learning and development program and achieve c 80% participation.
3. Provide c 2 opportunities for employees to work on passion projects per year.
4. Host c 1 internal hackathon per quarter.
5. Achieve a retention rate of c 95% for high-performing employees.

Web design and development company.

Objective: **Transform our website into a lead generation machine.**
Key Results:
1. Increase website traffic by 50% within 6 months.
2. Increase conversion rate from website visitor to lead by 25% within 6 months.
3. Implement 5 new lead generation tactics.
4. Achieve a lead-to-customer conversion rate of 15%.
5. Achieve a customer acquisition cost of no more than $100.

Objective: **Become the go-to agency for innovative website design.**
Key Results:
1. Launch 2 new website design offerings.
2. Achieve a project profitability of 30%.
3. Win 3 industry awards for website design.
4. Present 1 web design-related talk at an industry conference.
5. Achieve a customer retention rate of 95%.

Manufacturing company.

Objective: **Become a zero-waste facility.**
Key Results:
1. Achieve a recycling rate of 95%.
2. Develop and implement a plan to repurpose or reuse 75% of waste materials.
3. Achieve a landfill diversion rate of 98%.
4. Launch a new product line made from repurposed waste materials.
5. Partner with 1 other company to jointly achieve zero waste goals.

Objective: **Increase customer satisfaction by 50%.**
Key Results:
1. Conduct a customer satisfaction survey and implement 3 improvements based on feedback.
2. Achieve a customer retention rate of 95%.
3. Launch a new customer loyalty program.
4. Respond to all customer inquiries within 1 hour during business hours.
5. Achieve a Net Promoter Score of 9 out of 10.

Non-profit organization.

Objective: **Double the impact of our programs.**
Key Results:
1. Increase the number of individuals served by our programs by 50% within 1 year.
2. Increase the number of community partnerships by 25% within 6 months.
3. Achieve a program satisfaction rate of at least 95%.
4. Increase the number of volunteer hours by 50% within 1 year.
5. Secure 3 major grants to fund program expansion.

Objective: **Become a thought leader in our industry.**
Key Results:
1. Publish 2 articles in industry publications.
2. Speak at 3 industry conferences.
3. Achieve a social media following of 10,000.
4. Host 1 industry-related event per quarter.
5. Achieve a media mention rate of 1 per month.

Retail company.

Objective: **Become the go-to destination for sustainable fashion.**
Key Results:
1. Increase sales of sustainable fashion products by 50% within 6 months.
2. Launch a new marketing campaign.
3. Achieve a sustainability-related social media following of 10,000.
4. Partner with 3 sustainable fashion brands.
5. Host 1 sustainability-focused event per quarter.

Objective: **Create a world-class customer experience.**
Key Results:
1. Implement a customer feedback system and act on 80% of customer feedback received.
2. Train all customer-facing employees on customer service best practices and track improvement in customer satisfaction scores.
3. Develop and launch a customer rewards program.
4. Roll out a new customer portal.
5. Achieve a Net Promoter Score of 9.

Logistics company.

Objective: **Create a fully automated and digitalized logistics process.**
Key Results:
1. Implement a new transportation management system and achieve a 50% reduction in shipping errors.
2. Launch a new online portal for customers to track shipments and place orders.
3. Achieve a paperless rate of 95%.
4. Implement 3 new automation technologies.
5. Achieve a customer retention rate of 95%.

Objective: **Expand into two new regions.**
Key Results:
1. Research and identify 2 potential new regions.
2. Secure 5 pilot customers in each new region.
3. Achieve a customer retention rate of 80% in each new region.
4. Achieve a profit margin of 15% in each new region.
5. Establish 1 strategic partnership in each new region.

Service company.

Objective: Become the go-to provider of XYZ services in our industry.
Key Results:
1. Increase market share by 10% within 1 year.
2. Launch 2 new service offerings.
3. Increase customer retention by 20% through the implementation of a new customer success program.
4. Attend 2 industry conferences and present on a panel or as a keynote speaker.
5. Achieve a Net Promoter Score of 9 out of 10.

Objective: Foster a culture of continuous learning and development.
Key Results:
1. Implement a new learning and development program and achieve 80% participation.
2. Provide 2 opportunities for employees to work on passion projects per year.
3. Host 1 internal hackathon per quarter.
4. Achieve a retention rate of 95% for high-performing employees.
5. Offer 3 professional development workshops per year.

Hospitality industry.

Objective: **Become the go-to destination for wellness retreats.**
Key Results:
1. Increase bookings for wellness retreats by 50% within 6 months.
2. Launch a new wellness retreat package.
3. Achieve a satisfaction rate of 95% for wellness retreat guests.
4. Partner with 3 wellness brands or practitioners.
5. Host 1 wellness-focused event per quarter.

Objective: **Create a world-class guest experience.**
Key Results:
1. Implement a guest feedback system and act on 80% of feedback received.
2. Train all guest-facing employees on customer service best practices and track improvement in guest satisfaction scores.
3. Develop and launch a guest rewards program.
4. Roll out a new, easy-to-use guest portal.
5. Achieve a Net Promoter Score of 9 out of 10.

Energy industry.

Objective: **Become a leader in renewable energy.**
Key Results:
1. Increase the percentage of renewable energy in our energy mix by 50%.
2. Launch 2 new renewable energy products or services.
3. Achieve a 20% reduction in greenhouse gas emissions.
4. Partner with 3 organizations or initiatives.
5. Host renewable energy-focused event.

Objective: **Create a world-class customer experience.**
Key Results:
1. Implement a customer feedback system and act on 80% of customer feedback received.
2. Train all customer-facing employees on customer service best practices and track improvement in customer satisfaction scores.
3. Develop and launch a customer rewards program.
4. Roll out a new, easy-to-use customer portal.

Wholesale company.

Objective: **Expand our product offering to include sustainable and eco-friendly products.**
Key Results:
1. Increase sales of sustainable and eco-friendly products by 50%.
2. Launch a new sustainability-focused marketing campaign.
3. Achieve a sustainability-related social media following of 10,000.
4. Partner with 3 sustainable and eco-friendly brands.
5. Host 1 sustainability-focused event per quarter.

Objective: **Become the go-to provider of XYZ products in our industry.**
Key Results:
1. Increase market share by 10%.
2. Launch 2 new product lines.
3. Increase customer retention by 20% through the implementation of a new customer success program.
4. Attend 2 industry conferences and present on a panel or as a keynote speaker.
5. Achieve a Net Promoter Score of 9 out of 10.

Healthcare industry.

Objective: **Expand into two new service areas.**
Key Results:
1. Research and identify 2 potential new service areas.
2. Secure 5 pilot patients in each new service area.
3. Achieve a patient retention rate of 80% in each new service area.
4. Achieve a profit margin of 15% in each new service area.
5. Establish 1 strategic partnership in each new service area.

Objective: **Increase patient satisfaction by 50%.**
Key Results:
1. Conduct a patient satisfaction survey and implement 3 improvements based on feedback.
2. Achieve a patient retention rate of 95%.
3. Launch a new patient portal.
4. Respond to all patient inquiries within 1 hour during business hours.
5. Achieve a Net Promoter Score of 9 out of 10.

Agriculture.

Objective: **Increase crop yield by 25%.**
Key Results:
1. Implement precision farming techniques on 50% of our fields.
2. Increase the use of cover crops and organic fertilizers by 50%.
3. Reduce water usage by 20%.
4. Achieve a profit margin of 15%.
5. Launch 2 new high-yield crop varieties.

Objective: **Develop a new line of value-added products.**
Key Results:
1. Research and identify 3 potential value-added products.
2. Develop and test prototypes of 2 value-added products.
3. Launch 1 new value-added product.
4. Achieve a profit margin of 30% for value-added products.
5. Increase sales of value-added products by 50%.

Construction.

Objective: Increase the project completion rate by 25%.
Key Results:
1. Implement a new project management software and achieve a 20% reduction in project delays.
2. Achieve a project profit margin of 15%.
3. Secure 3 major contracts.
4. Increase customer satisfaction by 25% through the implementation of a new customer communication system.
5. Achieve a retention rate of 95% for high-performing employees.

Objective: Become a leader in sustainable construction practices.
Key Results:
1. Increase the use of recycled and eco-friendly materials by 50%.
2. Achieve a 20% reduction in construction waste.
3. Launch a new sustainability-focused marketing campaign.
4. Achieve a sustainability-related social media following of 10,000.
5. Host 1 sustainability-focused event per quarter.

Education.

Objective: **Increase student achievement by 25%.**
Key Results:
1. Implement a new curriculum and achieve a 20% improvement in test scores.
2. Increase the number of extracurricular programs offered by 50%.
3. Achieve a student retention rate of 95%.
4. Increase parent involvement by 25%.
5. Achieve a Net Promoter Score of 9 out of 10 for students, parents, and teachers.

Objective: **Become a leader in technology-enhanced learning.**
Key Results:
1. Increase the number of classrooms with interactive whiteboards by 50%.
2. Achieve a 20% increase in the use of online resources.
3. Train 80% of teachers on the use of technology in the classroom.
4. Launch a new online learning platform.
5. Achieve a satisfaction rate of 95% for online learners.

Finance.

Objective: **Increase revenue by 50%.**
Key Results:
1. Achieve a 50% increase in customer acquisition.
2. Increase average transaction value by 25%.
3. Launch 2 new financial products or services.
4. Increase customer retention by 20%.
5. Achieve a profit margin of 30%.

Objective: **Expand into 2 new regions.**
Key Results:
1. Research and identify 2 potential new regions.
2. Secure 5 pilot customers in each new region.
3. Achieve a customer retention rate of 80% in each new region.
4. Achieve a profit margin of 15% in each new region.
5. Establish 1 strategic partnership in each new region.

Government.

Objective: **Increase citizen satisfaction by 25%.**
Key Results:
1. Implement a new citizen feedback system and act on 80% of feedback received.
2. Increase the number of online services offered by 50%.
3. Achieve a satisfaction rate of 95% for online services.
4. Increase citizen participation in community events by 25%.
5. Achieve a Net Promoter Score of 9 out of 10 for citizens.

Objective: **Reduce the cost of government operations by 15%.**
Key Results:
1. Implement 3 cost-saving initiatives.
2. Achieve a 10% reduction in energy usage.
3. Achieve a 10% reduction in paper usage.
4. Achieve a 10% reduction in travel costs.
5. Achieve a 10% reduction in supplies and materials costs.

Legal.

Objective: Increase billable hours by 25%.
Key Results:
1. Increase the number of new clients by 50%.
2. Achieve a retention rate of 95% for high-performing clients.
3. Launch 2 new legal services.
4. Achieve a profit margin of 30%.
5. Attend 2 industry conferences and present on a panel or as a keynote speaker.

Objective: Foster a culture of continuous learning and development.
Key Results:
1. Implement a new learning and development program and achieve 80% participation.
2. Provide 2 opportunities for employees to work on passion projects per year.
3. Host 1 internal hackathon per quarter.
4. Achieve a retention rate of 95% for high-performing employees.
5. Offer 3 professional development workshops per year.

Marketing.

Objective: **Increase website traffic by 50%.**
Key Results:
1. Implement a new search engine optimization strategy and achieve a 50% increase in organic traffic.
2. Launch 2 new marketing campaigns.
3. Increase social media following by 50%.
4. Achieve a 10% conversion rate for website visitors.
5. Attend 2 industry conferences and present on a panel or as a keynote speaker.

Objective: **Increase brand awareness by 25%.**
Key Results:
1. Launch a new brand marketing campaign.
2. Achieve a brand mention rate of 1 per week in industry publications.
3. Increase social media following by 50%.
4. Host 1 brand-building event

Real estate.

Objective: **Increase property sales by 50%.**
Key Results:
1. Increase the number of new listings by 25%.
2. Achieve a retention rate of 95% for high-performing agents.
3. Launch a new property sales marketing campaign.
4. Achieve a conversion rate of 10% for leads.
5. Attend 2 industry conferences and present on a panel or as a keynote speaker.

Objective: **Expand into 2 new markets.**
Key Results:
1. Research and identify 2 potential new markets.
2. Secure 5 pilot listings in each new market.
3. Achieve a property sales conversion rate of 8% in each new market.
4. Achieve a profit margin of 15% in each new market.
5. Establish 1 strategic partnership in each new market.

Transportation.

Objective: **Increase delivery efficiency by 25%.**
Key Results:
1. Implement a new delivery routing software and achieve a 20% reduction in delivery times.
2. Increase the use of environmentally-friendly vehicles by 50%.
3. Achieve a retention rate of 95% for high-performing drivers.
4. Increase customer satisfaction by 25% through the implementation of a new tracking system.
5. Achieve a Net Promoter Score of 9 out of 10 for customers.

Objective: **Expand into 2 new regions.**
Key Results:
1. Research and identify 2 potential new regions.
2. Secure 5 pilot customers in each new region.
3. Achieve a customer retention rate of 80% in each new region.
4. Achieve a profit margin of 15% in each new region.
5. Establish 1 strategic partnership in each new region.

Utilities.

Objective: **Increase renewable energy usage by 50%.**
Key Results:
1. Increase the percentage of renewable energy in our energy mix by 50%.
2. Launch 2 new renewable energy products or services.
3. Achieve a 20% reduction in greenhouse gas emissions.
4. Partner with 3 renewable energy-focused organizations or initiatives.
5. Host 1 renewable energy-focused event.

Objective: **Create a world-class customer experience.**
Key Results:
1. Implement a customer feedback system and act on 80% of customer feedback received.
2. Train all customer-facing employees on customer service best practices and track improvement in customer satisfaction scores.
3. Develop and launch a customer rewards program.
4. Roll out a new, easy-to-use customer portal.

Mistakes in the formulation of OKR

While effective use of OKRs can drive company growth and success, it is important to avoid common pitfalls in order to get the most benefit from the framework. Let's delve into some of the most common mistakes organizations make when formulating their OKRs.

Using a notional objective, more of a procedure or slogan: Using a goal that is too vague or general, such as "perform our job better," is a common error in the creation of OKRs. This makes it challenging to comprehend and track progress toward achieving it. Instead, the goal should be clear and measurable, like "become the best company in XYZ in terms of customer satisfaction."

Another common mistake is to use **key results that are hard to measure or have vague meanings**, like "increase team morale." Because of this, it can be hard for team members to understand what is expected of them and how they can help reach the goal. Instead, the most important results should be clear and measurable, like "plan team-building events once a week" or "evaluate team morale once a month."

Include indicators that are extremely lagging. Leading indicators that can be used to predict future success are just as important as trailing indicators for measuring the progress of a goal. For example, if the goal is to "raise sales revenue by 20%," the total sales revenue at the end of the quarter could be a lagging indicator, while the number of leads created each week could be a leading indicator. If all of the most important results are lagging indicators, it might be too late to change book if the goal is not being met.

The objective is not equal to the total of the key results: Key results must support and contribute to the achievement of the overall objective. If not all of the key results help reach the goal, the OKR may need to be reevaluated and changed. For example, if the goal is to "launch a new product," important results could include the end of market research, the completion of the product design, and the acquisition of funding.

Too many goals or key results: Too many goals or key results might distract team members and make it challenging for them to prioritize their jobs. It's important to keep the number of OKRs in check and focus on a small number of very effective goals. For instance, it might be more productive to concentrate on 1-3 core objectives for the quarter rather than setting 10 goals.

Although OKRs are designed to be a flexible and adaptable framework for goal-setting, it's vital to keep in mind that they do not serve as a **replacement for conventional project management** techniques. To be successful, it's important to keep a clear line between the two and use them both at the same time. For example, project management techniques can be used to break down key results into smaller, more manageable tasks or initiatives that can be done.

Checklist for OKR self-verification

- ✓ Limit the number of objectives to one to three per division or organization to help you stay focused and avoid multitasking.

- ✓ Set three to five Key Results for each Objective to prioritize your efforts and make sure you are making progress.

- ✓ To align your Objectives and Key Results, ensure that each Objective is binary, with no room for doubt about whether it has been met.

- ✓ Use the term "quarterly completion" to make sure each Objective can be completed within a quarter, helping you stay on track and make progress.

- ✓ Make sure each Key Result can be measured weekly to track your progress and identify areas where you may need to adjust your approach.

- ✓ Allow Key Results to change on a weekly basis if needed to adapt to changing circumstances and stay focused on achieving your objectives.

- ✓ Ensure that Key Results can be changed in parallel, rather than in a serial or sequential manner, to stay agile and responsive to changing circumstances.

- ✓ Make sure each Key Result contributes either to the purpose of the company or to the goals of neighboring teams to align with your organization's overall goals.

- ✓ Set the duration of Key Results to be the same, equal to a quarter, to stay focused on the task at hand and avoid getting sidetracked.

- ✓ Ensure that your Objective is equal to the sum of your Key Results to stay focused on your overall goals and make progress towards achieving them.

- ✓ Make sure your Objective sound inspiring or at least interesting to stay motivated and engaged in the process of achieving them.

What to do next

How to present your OKR to colleagues and team

Making a video presentation of your OKR (Objectives and Key Results) is a great way to share them with your coworkers and team. This can be especially useful if your team is spread out geographically or if you simply want to be sure the OKR gets across and sticks with everyone.

Here are some guidelines for developing a compelling OKR presentation:

1. Capture a video of your computer screen using a webcam, and you may not only show your OKR to your team but also talk about why you choose each objective and KR. For simultaneous screen and webcam recording on a laptop, you can use programmes like Loom, Vimeo, Quicktime, or the Win+G keyboard shortcut on laptop.

2. Don't go over 5 minutes and be sure to get right to the subject. This will keep your staff interested in and attentive to the presentation material.

3. Define your terms and be specific about your goals and the outcomes you expect to see: Make sure you explain why you're setting each goal and how you expect to use the outcomes to succeed.

4. Drive home the value of the OKRs by highlighting their significance to the group and the company as a whole.

5. Slides, charts, and other visual aids can help illustrate your arguments and keep the audience interested in what you have to say.

6. A video presentation is a great way to introduce new team members and share your OKR with the group. To help new team members get up to speed and start contributing right away, consider recording a presentation outlining the team's aims and expectations and sharing it with them.

A recommended outline for your OKR presentation is as follows:

1. Start by explaining why you're giving this presentation and giving a brief summary of the OKR.

2. Next, think about what you want to accomplish. To kick things off, clarify the objective's language and its significance to the overarching aims of the team and the firm.

3. Next, you should elaborate on the benefits that will accrue to your team and the company as a whole from achieving this goal. How will the group and the company profit from succeeding at this goal?

4. Key Results: Describe the weekly metrics that will be used to track each key result. Is there a source from which we can expect data?

5. At the end of your presentation, it's a good idea to go through the OKR as a whole again and stress

their significance to your team. Remind them how important it is to not lose sight of their goals and to keep their focus and dedication strong.

It's important to make the presentation concise and to the point and to use visuals to back up your claims whenever possible. This format will make it easy for you to explain your OKR to your team and make sure that everyone has the same idea of what you want to happen.

Here you can see example of presentation:

Presentor: XXXXXXXX

OKR for XXXXXX department for Q4 2019

Achieve Next Level

- Reduce expenses on one story-point to XX$
- For every MR CI/CD Manifest should be done
- 90% working time should be billed to client projects
- Level of business effectiveness to be increase up to 60

What do we mean by this

List here the description of the Goal.
What you mean by such word choice, what is packed inside

What is in this goal for us?

Why have you chosen such Goal?
How department and company will benefit from reaching it?

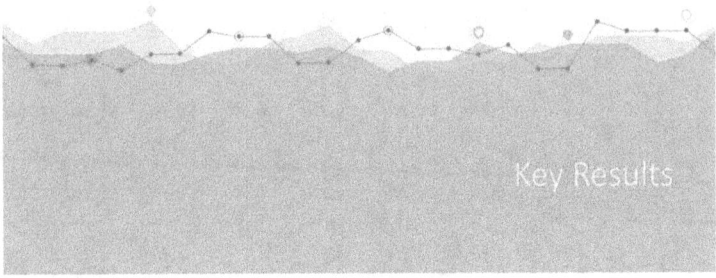
Key Results

KR 1. Reduce expenses on one story-point to XX$

How will we measure this on weekly basis
Where numbers will be taken from

What are the current numbers

Achieve Next Level

- Reduce expenses on one story-point to XX$
- For every MR CI/CD Manifest should be done
- 90% working time should be billed to client projects
- Level of business effectiveness to be increase up to 60

What to do next with OKR inside your team

Companies often find it hard to use Objectives and Key Results (OKR) with each employee because it can be hard for employees to come up with their own OKRs this requires time and skill. Because of this, OKR is often only used at the team level, and it is up to the manager to share the team's goals and key results with the team. One way to use OKR on a team level is to have each team member fill out a spreadsheet with their goals, key results, and the tasks they will do to help reach those key results.

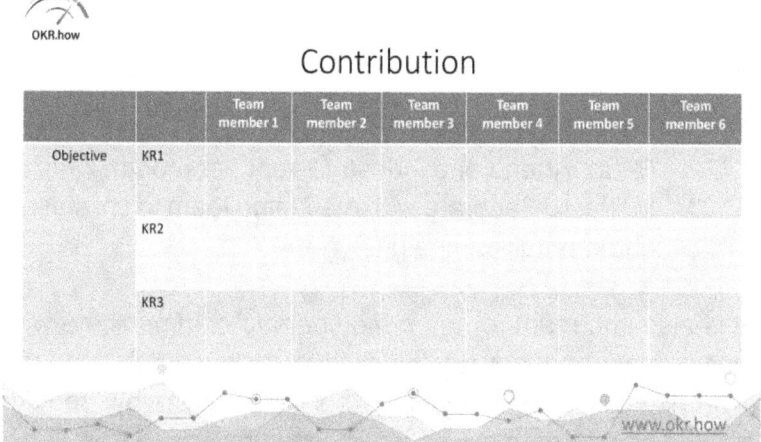

For example, a manager might bring a spreadsheet to the team with the goal of increasing sales by 25% in the next quarter. The team might then fill out the spreadsheet with their key results and tasks, such as:

Team Members:
1. Vasyl
2. Petro
3. Maria

Goals:
Increase sales by 25%
Key Results:
1. Make at least 10 sales calls per day.
2. Attend two industry events per month to network with potential customers.
3. Collaborate with the marketing team to create targeted email campaigns having 10 meetings.

Tasks:

1. Vasyl: Make at least 5 sales calls per day.
2. Petro: Attend one industry event per month.
3. Maria: Collaborate with marketing team to create targeted email campaigns.

It is also important for team members to communicate with each other about how their individual tasks contribute to the overall goals of the company. This can be done by creating a table where team members list what they need from each other in order to achieve their key results. For example, if Vasyl needs Petro to provide them with a list of potential clients in order to make sales calls, they can list that on the table. Team members can help each other reach their goals if they agree on these requests and promises.

Facilitation

	Team member 1	Team member 2	Team member 3	Team member 4	Team member 5	Team member 6
Team member 1	■					
Team member 2		■				
Team member 3			■			
Team member 4				■		
Team member 5					■	
Team member 6						■

Teams should look over and talk about their OKR regularly to make sure they are on track to meet their goals. This can be done through weekly or monthly check-ins, where team members review their progress and make any necessary adjustments to their plans. By regularly reviewing and discussing OKR, teams can stay focused and make sure they are making progress towards their goals.

OKR tracking

How to track your OKR

Tracking Objectives and Key Results (OKR) has several benefits, including:

1. **Improved focus:** By regularly reviewing and tracking OKR, teams and individuals can stay focused on the goals that they have set for themselves and make sure they are making progress towards achieving them.

2. **Increased accountability:** When OKR are tracked publicly, team members are more likely to stay accountable for their progress and work harder to achieve their goals.

3. **Greater transparency:** Publicly tracking OKR can also increase transparency within a team or organization, as everyone can see the progress being made towards the company's goals.

4. **Enhanced communication:** Tracking OKR can also improve communication within a team or organization, as it allows team members to discuss their progress and identify any challenges or obstacles that need to be addressed.

Regular OKR (Objectives and Key Results) check meetings are an important tool for companies to track progress towards their goals and make any necessary adjustments along the way. These meetings should be held at least once a week in order to stay up-to-date on progress and make timely adjustments. Less frequent meetings, such as once every two weeks or once a month, might not provide the right amount of oversight and might slow down progress toward the OKRs.

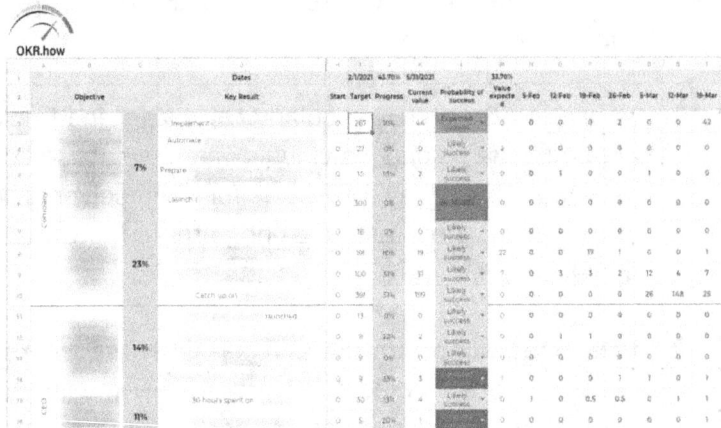

During these check meetings, it is important to review the progress that has been made towards achieving the key results that have been set. This could mean looking at data and metrics, talking about any problems that have come up, and thinking about whether the strategies being used to reach the OKRs need to be changed in any way. Also, the OKRs themselves may need to be looked at and possibly changed if they are no longer realistic or useful.

In addition to the weekly check meetings, it may also be useful to have a monthly "control slice" meeting to take a broader view of the company's progress towards its OKRs. This meeting can be used to check that the strategies being used to achieve the OKRs are still up-to-date and effective, and to review and adapt the OKRs themselves if needed. By reviewing its plans often and making changes as needed, a company can stay on track to reach its goals and make any book corrections that are needed along the way.

Here are some tips for tracking OKRs:

Use traffic light colors to show progress. For example, you could use red, yellow, and green to show how each key result is going. Red could indicate that progress is behind schedule, yellow could indicate that progress is on track, and green could indicate that the key result has been achieved.

Track progress on both the key result and time. It's important to track progress on both the key result itself and the amount of time that has passed. If the progress on the key result is further along in percentage compared to the progress on time, it indicates that the company is on track to achieve the key result. If the progress on the key result is less in percentage compared to the progress on time, it indicates that the company may be falling behind and may need to change its approach.

Use graphs to see progress. Think about using graphs to show how each key result is changing over time. This can help make it easier to see how well the company is doing and identify any areas that may need more attention.

Be proactive about addressing any issues. If the progress of a key result is falling behind, it's important to be proactive about addressing the issue. This may involve changing the approach being used, adjusting the key result itself, or providing additional resources to help the team achieve the key result.

To make sure that regular OKR check-in meetings are productive and effective, there are a few things to avoid:

1. **Don't turn them into a bureaucracy**: OKR check-ins should be a way to synchronize and align efforts, not a ritual or bureaucracy. Avoid turning them into a way of simply reporting on what has been done.

2. **Avoid unnecessary details**: It's important to focus on the key results and progress towards achieving them, rather than getting bogged down in irrelevant details.

3. **Don't train public speaking when there is nothing to say**: Only speak up if you have something meaningful to contribute to the discussion.

4. **Recognize the importance of check-ins for development**: OKR check-ins should be seen as an opportunity for development and improvement, not just a way to report on progress.

5. **Rotate the host role**: Consider rotating the role of host among team members to ensure that everyone has an opportunity to lead the discussion and facilitate the meeting.

6. **Be willing to change strategies if necessary**: If the current strategy for achieving a goal is not working, don't be afraid to consider alternative approaches.

7. **Don't ignore what is visible from the outside**: Make sure to consider external factors and how they

may be impacting the company's progress towards its OKRs.

And I need to mention whistleblowers. In the context of OKR (Objectives and Key Results) check-ins, a whistleblower may be a team member who brings attention to any issues or problems that could impact the company's ability to achieve its goals. This could include things like being unethical, doing things that are against the law, or not following the rules.

It is important for companies to create a safe and supportive environment where whistleblowers feel comfortable coming forward with their concerns. During OKR check-ins, the person in charge should make sure that everyone feels welcome and free to share their ideas and concerns. This can help make sure that any problems or issues are brought to light and fixed quickly.

ORDER IN CHAOS by Kostiantyn Koptelov

EVALUATION ALGORITHM OKR

OPTION I
CLASSICAL

- SINGLE SCALE OKR SCORE WHERE 0 - NOT REACHED AT ALL, AND 1 - 100% COMPLETED

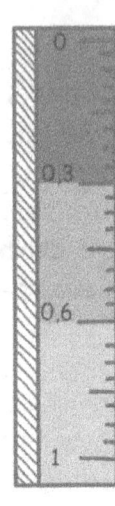

OPTION II
USING OF TWO SCORING SYSTEMS

FIRST RATING SCALE
OBJECTIVE
- OKR ACHIEVEMENT ASSESSMENT ACCORDING TO THE CLASSIC VERSION

SECOND RATING SCALE
SUBJECTIVE
- ASSESSMENT MADE BY THE OWNER OF KR, WHO DIRECTLY REACHED IT

MAKES IT POSSIBLE TO CORRELATE RESULTS AND FORM MORE SPECIFIC GOAL

OPTION III
AUTHOR'S

- ENCLOSED IN THE NAVIGATION SYSTEM ON REACHING THE GOAL

- RESULTS ACHIEVEMENT RULER

- POSSIBILITY TO CONTROL WHAT WE DID AND FOR HOW LONG IT TOOK

- TIME RULER FOR RESULTS

*READ MORE ABOUT THE ALGORITHM AT
WWW.OKR.HOW

Weekly OKR meeting

Weekly OKR (Objectives and Key Results) check-ins let businesses track their progress toward their goals and make any required adjustments along the way. It is critical to follow certain best practices in order to make these check-ins as productive and effective as possible.

Prior to the meeting:

1. Check that everyone has updated the tracking tool (such as a table, spreadsheet, or software used to track OKRs) with the most up-to-date information on their OKRs.
2. Before the meeting, encourage team members to fill out a general presentation or send a status report to the general chat. This can assist in ensuring that everyone is ready to engage in the check-in.

Meeting structure:

1. The meeting's focus should be on reconciliation rather than discussion. Team members should provide updates on the status of their main results as well as any challenges or roadblocks that have developed. Team members are usually allowed no more than 5 minutes to present and answer questions.
2. To keep the group focused and on track, the facilitator should ask clear, resolved questions such as "yes/no/number".
3. If there are more in-depth concerns or roadblocks that necessitate brainstorming or more extensive research, it is preferable to plan another meeting and invite only relevant team members, rather than

waste everyone's time. Meetings may be huge time wasters, therefore it is critical to plan ahead of time and stick to a precise schedule and timetable.
4. Consider employing screen sharing so that everyone in the meeting can see each other's status.

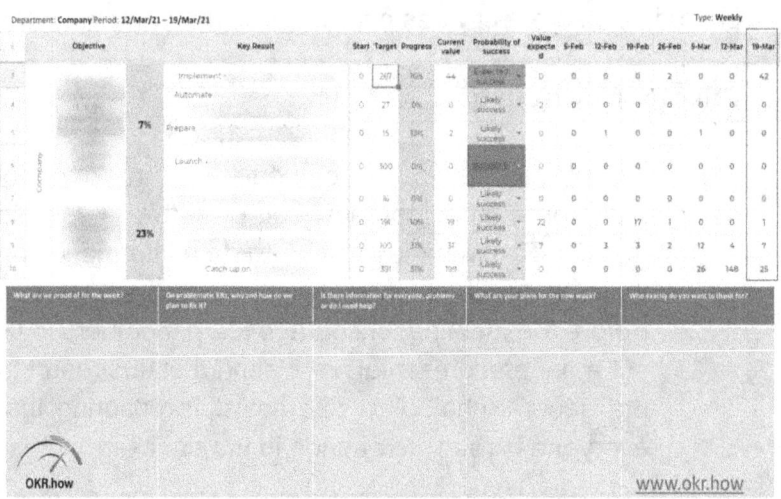

Reporting questions for the meeting:

1. **What can we be proud of this week? What was done in general to achieve the objectives?** This helps the team reflect on their accomplishments and share their progress with the rest of the organization. For example, the marketing team may be proud of the number of leads they generated, while the sales team may be proud of the number of deals they closed.
2. **Why and how are we going to fix the problematic key results?** This helps the team identify any issues or challenges they are facing and develop a plan to get back on track. For example, If a team's key result

of increasing website traffic by 20% over the quarter is not on track, they should identify the reasons why and come up with strategies to improve their performance. Possible solutions might include creating more engaging social media content, launching targeted ad campaigns, or creating a content calendar to regularly publish new content on the website. By implementing targeted solutions, the team can work to get back on track and achieve their key result.

3. **Is there any information for everyone, any announcements, any problems, or do I require assistance?** This helps the team stay informed and up-to-date on any relevant news or issues that may impact their work.

4. **What are your overall plans for the upcoming week?** This ensures that everyone is on the same page and focused on the most critical priorities and goals. Setting clear goals and priorities for the following week allows the team to stay focused and make progress toward their goals.

5. **Who do you wish to thank for their help? Kudos.** It is also important to thank team members who have contributed to the team's success, such as an employee who worked extra hours to meet a deadline or a group of employees who worked together to achieve a goal. By thanking those who have helped, teams can stay motivated to achieve their objectives.

It's also a good idea to alternate the facilitator job among team members so that everyone has a chance to lead the discussion and facilitate the meeting. By following these best practices, companies may be able to make their weekly OKR check-ins more productive and useful.

Monthly OKR meeting

Monthly reconciliation of OKR (Objectives and Key Results) is an important way to make sure that the company's goals and strategies are on track and in line with reality. During the reconciliation process, the CEO should start by looking at the goals and making sure they are in line with what is happening. This could mean looking over the materials from the strategic session to see if there are any differences. For example, if the target is to increase conversions by 10%, the CEO may review data on the number of conversions and compare it to the target to see if the company is on track.

It is also important to check for any "double KRs," where the name is the same, but the metrics are different. This can help ensure that the company is measuring progress consistently and accurately. For example, if one team is measuring the success of a marketing campaign by the number of leads generated, while another team is measuring the same campaign by the number of conversions, this could lead to confusion and inaccurate reporting.

If there are any important signs that show the company isn't on track to reach its goals, the approach may need to be changed. This could mean changing the goal or key result or taking care of any problems that are stopping the company from moving forward. For example, if the company doesn't get the help or resources it needs from other teams or contractors, it might not be able to reach some of its goals, and it needs to change its strategy toward those goals. In the same way, if an objective or key result isn't good enough or doesn't matter, it might need to be changed.

I recommend making monthly syncs public and inviting all company employees, usually in a mode where they can only listen but can ask questions in the chat. This can help ensure that everyone is informed and aligned with the company's goals and progress. Each team should report on what has been achieved in general terms, highlight any contributions that deserve recognition, and discuss any key results that are not in the green zone.

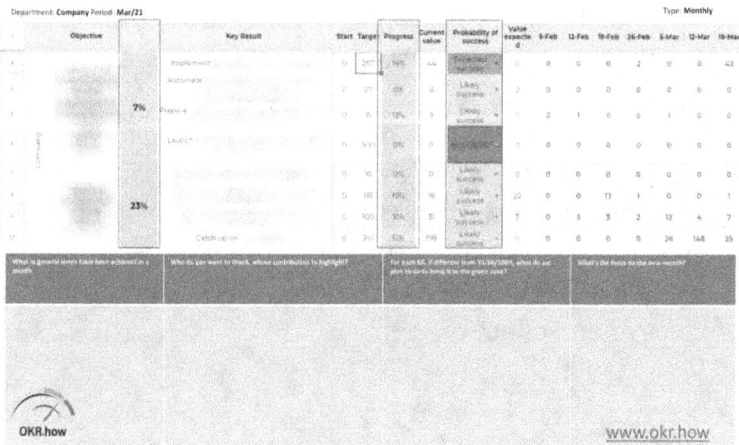

Questions to be reported by every team during the meeting:

1. **What in general terms have been achieved in a month?** This can help the company understand how each team is contributing to the overall goals and progress of the organization.
2. **Who do you want to thank, whose contribution to highlight?** This can help motivate and engage team members and foster a positive team culture.
3. **For each KR, if different from 33/66/100%, what do we plan to do to bring it to the green zone?** By discussing any key results that are not in the green

zone, the team can identify any issues or challenges and develop a plan to get back on track.
4. **What's the focus for the new month?** This can help ensure that the team is aligned and focused on the most important priorities and goals. For example, the marketing team may focus on improving the conversion rate for a specific campaign, or the sales team may focus on closing a high-priority deal. By setting clear goals and priorities for the coming month, the team can stay focused and make progress towards achieving their objectives.

By making the monthly sync public and inviting all employees to take part, the company can make sure that everyone knows about the company's goals and progress and is on the same page. By following these best practices, companies can make sure that their monthly OKR reconciliation is productive and effective.

Getting more from your OKR

What are the key thoughts to get more from OKRs

Here are some tips on how to get more out of OKR:

Keep track and pay attention to signals.

To get the most out of OKR, it is important to regularly track progress and pay attention to signals that may indicate the need for adjustments. By paying attention to these signals, teams can identify when they are off track and make necessary adjustments to get back on track.

1. At the end of each month, the team reviews their key results and compares them to their targets. If they are falling behind, they identify the reasons why and make adjustments to their strategies to get back on track.
2. The team uses a dashboard tool to visualize their progress on key results in real-time. This allows them to identify any trends or patterns that may indicate the need for adjustments.

Remind yourself and the team that ambitious goals can only be reached through ambitious strategies.

OKR is all about setting ambitious goals and striving to achieve them. It is important to remind yourself and your team that these goals are achievable and that the only way to reach them is through ambitious strategies and hard work. Encourage your team to think outside the box and question the way things are done so they can come up with new ways to reach their goals.

1. The team holds a brainstorming session to come up with new and innovative ideas for achieving their goals. They challenge each other to think outside the box and push the boundaries of what is possible.
2. The team leader regularly reminds the team of the importance of setting ambitious goals and encourages them to take calculated risks in order to achieve them.

Perform regular coaching and meetings on how team members are achieving their goals.

Regular coaching and meetings can help team members stay focused and motivated. They can also give teams a chance to talk about any problems or obstacles that are getting in the way of them reaching their goals. These sessions can be used to revise strategies or brainstorm new ideas to get back on track.

1. The team leader holds one-on-one coaching sessions with each team member to discuss their progress and any challenges they may be facing. They also provide feedback and guidance to help team members stay on track.
2. The team holds regular meetings to discuss their progress and any issues that may be impacting their ability to achieve their goals. These meetings provide an opportunity for team members to ask questions, share ideas, and get support from their colleagues.

Always strive to reach 100% of the goal, even if it is stretched.

While it is important to set realistic goals, it is also important to stretch yourself and your team to achieve as much as possible. Remember that we were discussing stretched and regular goals where applicable. This can be done by setting key results that are challenging but achievable and by constantly seeking ways to improve and do more. Even if you don't reach 100% of your goal, the effort to get there will drive progress and help your team achieve more in the long run.

1. The team sets key results that are challenging but achievable, and constantly seeks ways to improve and do more. The team holds regular meetings to brainstorm and find new strategies to achieve their goals.
2. Even if the team falls short of their goal, they review their progress and identify areas for improvement in order to do better next time. They also celebrate their achievements, no matter how small, as a way to stay motivated and focused on their goals.

Celebrate successes.

Celebrating successes along the way is another important tip for getting more out of OKR. Don't wait until the end of the quarter or year to celebrate your successes. Doing so can make you lose motivation and stop you from making progress. Instead, make it a point to celebrate your progress along the way. This can help keep your team focused and motivated, and it can also give them a morale boost when things get tough.

Here are some ways to celebrate your accomplishments:

1. Throw a party or lunch for your team to celebrate a big milestone or win.
2. Recognize each team member for what they did to help the team succeed.
3. Share your accomplishments with the rest of the company to show how far you've come.
4. Take a break and do something fun as a group to celebrate your success.

By making it a habit to celebrate your wins, you can keep your team motivated and interested, which will help you get better results and reach your OKRs.

In conclusion, to get the most out of OKR, you need to track progress regularly, remind yourself and your team that ambitious goals can be reached with ambitious strategies, coach and meet regularly, and always try to reach 100% of the goal. By following these tips, teams can effectively use OKR to drive progress and achieve their objectives.

How to identify need and apply changes to your OKR

To identify the need for changes to your OKRs, you can follow these steps:

1. **Review your current OKRs**: Take a look at the goals you have set for yourself and your team. Are they still relevant and aligned with your organization's overall mission and strategy?

2. **Assess your progress**. Look at how you and your team are progressing towards your OKRs. Are you making the progress you had hoped for? Are there any obstacles or challenges that are hindering your progress?

3. **Gather feedback**: Talk to your team members and stakeholders to get their input on your OKRs. Are they realistic and achievable? Please note that goals can be ambitious and stretched but still realistic. Are they aligned with the needs and goals of the organization and your team?

4. **Identify areas for improvement**: Based on your review, progress assessment, and feedback, identify areas where you can make changes to your OKRs to improve your chances of success.

To apply changes to your OKRs, follow these steps:

1. **Identify what has changed**: Determine what factors or circumstances have changed that warrant a revision of your OKRs.

2. **Communicate the changes**: Clearly communicate the changes you are making to your OKRs to your team and any relevant stakeholders.

3. **Set new key results**: Revise the key results associated with your OKRs to reflect the changes you have made. Make sure they are clear and measurable.

4. **Consider the potential impact of the changes**: Think about how the changes you are making to your OKRs may affect your team and other stakeholders.

How to make a retrospective on your OKRs

A meeting called a "retrospective" is where a group of people get together to reflect on their previous efforts and talk about how they may do better in the future. When a project is finished or when the quarter comes to a close, it is common practice to hold this event. In the framework of OKRs (Objectives and Key Results), the following are the procedures that should be taken when performing a retrospective:

1. **Establish an objective for the discussion.** The aim of the meeting should be to determine what aspects went well, what aspects may use some improvement, and how to proceed.

2. **Collect data.** Ask team members what they did and what they learned during the quarter. This data and feedback should include metrics like progress on important results as well as subjective feedback on team dynamics, communication, and other things.

3. **Find patterns**. Analyzing the data and the feedback to find patterns and themes will help you figure out what the themes are. These might involve victories as well as difficulties.

4. **Come up with some ideas** for how the team may enhance their performance in the future by basing them on the common themes that have surfaced during the brainstorming session. Changes like these might be made to procedures, tools, or even the dynamic of the team.

5. **Prioritize and plan**. Rank the ideas for improvement based on their potential impact and whether or not they are feasible, and then write a strategy for putting the top priorities into action based on your rankings.

6. **Follow-up**. Maintain a record of the action items that come out of the retrospective, and monitor the progress being made towards improving the problems that were identified.

During a retrospective for a software development team, for example, the team might decide that their biggest problem was that they didn't communicate well enough with each other. This discovery would take place during the retrospective. They might come up with ideas, like using a new project management tool or holding daily stand-up meetings, for how to improve communication. Then, they'd rank the best ideas and get ready to put them into action.

How to implement OKR in a company

The purpose of OKR implementation

The OKR (Objectives and Key Results) methodology not only helps organizations set and achieve specific goals, but it also has a significant impact on corporate culture. The process of implementing OKRs can lead to a transformation of the company as employees' and their relationships within the organization change and trust levels increase. OKRs can help create a more efficient and cohesive work environment.

When starting an OKR implementation project, it is essential to understand that it is not just about achieving numbers and metrics but also about building team spirit and improving communication. The process of putting OKRs into action is a big job, and it's important that management and top-level leaders are on board and understand how important the method is.

Be prepared for the specific challenges of goal-setting, management, and policy. The implementation of OKRs can lead to changes in employee interactions, and it is important to be aware that some employees may attempt to set each other up for new roles. It is important to be ready for this and to make sure that management knows about the possible changes and is ready to deal with them.

Also, the OKR implementation process can be used as a litmus test to find out where the company isn't working well and where employees have bad habits. Be prepared for this as well and be open to addressing and improving it.

Before deciding to implement OKRs (Objectives and Key Results), it is essential to understand the problem that the organization wants to solve with the tool. OKRs are a tool, and like any tool, they need to be used for a specific purpose. Without understanding the problem that the organization wants to solve, the implementation of OKRs can be ineffective.

It is important to take a step back and think about what the organization wants to achieve with OKRs. This could be something as simple as transparency or as complex as improving communication and involving employees in the decision-making process. The approach, layout, and consistency of the OKRs will be based on the needs of the organization.

When putting OKRs into place, it is important to know what the owner or board wants and expects. Sometimes, the owners may want the appearance of numbers and transparency but don't necessarily want employees to set their own targets. In these cases, the implementation of OKRs should be tailored to meet the specific needs of the organization.

Before putting OKRs into place, it is important to do an audit of the organization to get a full picture of how things are going. This will help find the specific business problem that OKRs will solve and make sure that the implementation is made to fit the needs of the organization.

In conclusion, OKRs are a powerful way to reach specific goals, but before deciding to use them, an organization needs to know what problem it wants to solve with them. Conducting an audit, understanding the owner's or board's goals and expectations, and choosing the single most important answer to the question, "Why do we need them?" will ensure the effective implementation of OKRs and bring benefits to the organization as a whole.

Gradual approach on OKR implementation

The best way to implement OKR (Objectives and Key Results) is in stages, starting with the top management level and working your way down to the rest of the company. This approach allows for a gradual implementation of the methodology, allowing for any adjustments to be made along the way.

The first quarter should focus on introducing OKRs to the top management level. This will give the implementation a strong base and make sure that the goals and key results are in line with the organization's overall vision and direction.

In the second quarter, focus on training the middle management level and encouraging them to attend regular monthly reconciliations. Not to report, but just to attend to get used to the OKRs. This will help make sure that the goals and key results are in line with how the organization works and what it does every day.

In the third quarter, focus on expanding the implementation to include both top and middle management levels. This will ensure that the objectives and key results are aligned across all levels of the organization and that all employees have a clear understanding of the OKR methodology.

Finally, in the fourth quarter, expand the implementation to include the entire company. This will make sure that all employees know about the OKR method and are able to help get the goals and key results met.

It is important to note that this phased approach is not set in stone and that it can be adjusted as needed depending on the specific needs of the organization. The most important thing is to start small and gradually expand the implementation to include the entire company. This phased approach will help to ensure a smooth implementation of the OKR methodology and will allow for any adjustments to be made along the way.

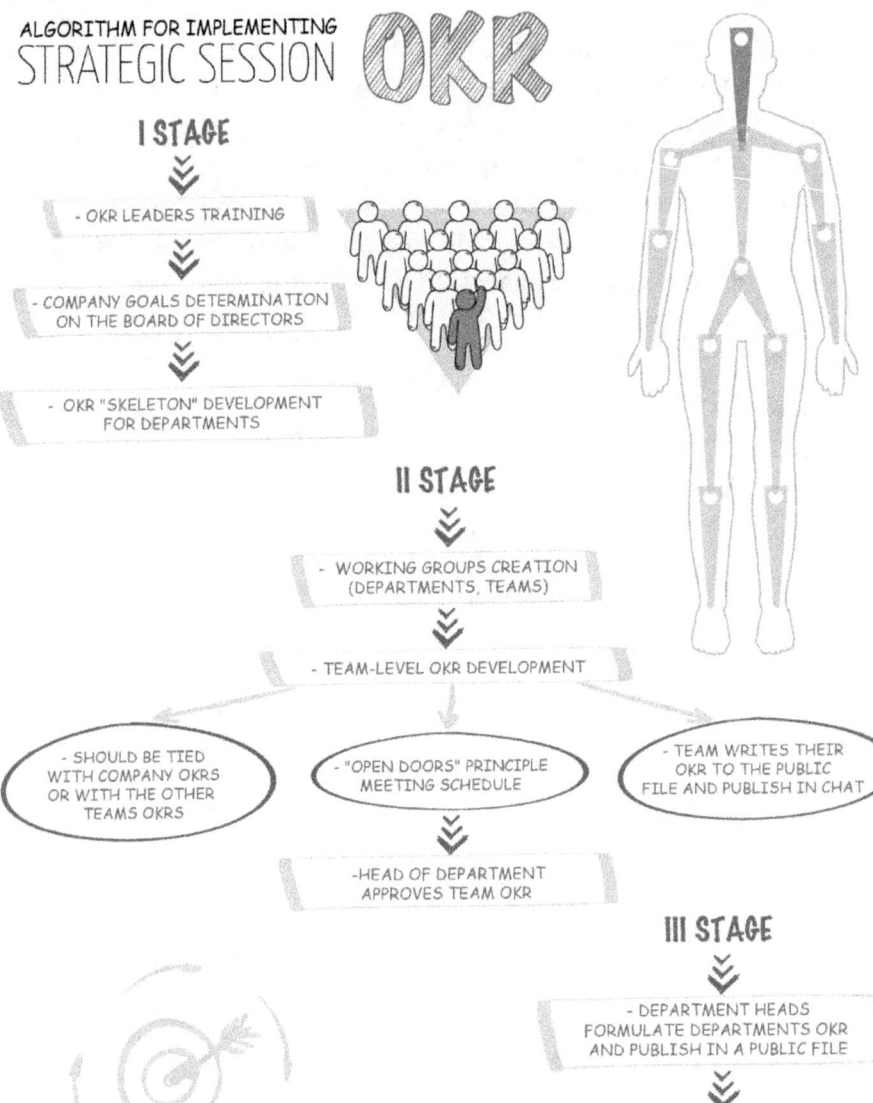

A step-by-step OKR implementation algorithm.

Implementing OKRs (Objectives and Key Results) in a company can be a powerful way to align teams and individuals around specific, measurable goals. But it's important to go into the process of implementation with a clear understanding of the company's needs and culture. The following steps can be used as a general outline for implementing OKRs:

Mini-audit before the project: Before starting to use OKRs, it's important to do a mini-audit to see if they're a good fit for the company. This step involves figuring out how the company is doing right now and what its specific needs and challenges are. By conducting a mini audit, we can identify areas where OKRs can be most beneficial and tailor the implementation process accordingly.

OKR in-depth training: Once it has been determined that OKRs are a good fit for the company, it is important to provide training for top management and OKR leaders. This step ensures that everyone involved in the implementation process understands the basics of OKRs and how to use them effectively. It is also important to provide training on the various tools and technologies that will be used to track and measure progress against OKRs.

Strategic session to formulate BHAG and OKR for a year and a quarter: After training, the next step is to hold strategic sessions to set BHAGs (big, hairy, audacious goals) and OKRs for the year and quarter. This step involves getting input from all stakeholders and using this information to create a shared vision for the company. By doing so, we can create specific and trackable goals that align with the company's overall strategy and objectives.

Strategic meeting to decompose quarterly OKRs on teams and align their goals: Once the OKRs have been established, the next step is to decompose the quarter OKRs into team-specific goals and align them. This step involves getting input from each team and working together to make sure that the goals support the overall company strategy and are in line with each other.

Building a habit for effective weekly and monthly check-ins: After the OKRs have been established and aligned across teams, it is important to establish regular check-ins to monitor progress and make adjustments as needed. These check-ins can be done weekly or monthly, depending on the needs of the company.

Retrospective: After a quarter has passed, it's important to have a retrospective to look back at how well the OKRs were put into place and find ways to make them better. This step can assist the company in determining what worked well and what didn't, so that adjustments can be made for the following quarter.

Planning next quarter: After the retrospective, the next step is to plan for the next quarter's OKRs. This step involves updating the OKRs that are already in place, setting new goals, and making sure that the goals are in line with the company's overall strategy.

Overall, implementing OKRs is a process that requires careful planning and execution. By following the steps above, companies can make sure that they can get teams and individuals to work toward clear, measurable goals and keep track of their progress. However, it is important to remember that this is a general process that may vary depending on the company's culture, size, and needs.

Common mistakes in OKR implementation

There are several common mistakes that companies can make when implementing OKRs (Objectives and Key Results):

Not involving all stakeholders in the process. OKRs are most effective when they align with the overall company strategy and objectives. If all stakeholders, which are usually all departments' directors or heads, are not involved in the process of setting OKRs, it can lead to goals that are not aligned with the company's overall direction.

Setting unrealistic goals. OKRs should be specific, measurable, and achievable, but they should also be ambitious. If the goals are not challenging enough, they may not inspire individuals and teams to put in the extra effort required to achieve them. On the other hand, if the goals are too unrealistic, they can demotivate teams and lead to frustration.

Not providing enough training and support. OKRs can be a powerful tool for aligning teams and individuals around specific, measurable, but ambitious goals. But if people don't know how to use OKRs effectively, they might not be able to get the results they want.

Not keeping track of progress and making changes. OKRs are living documents that should be looked at and changed often. If progress is not monitored and adjustments are not made, teams may not be able to achieve their goals.

Not conducting retrospectives. Retrospectives are an important step in the OKR implementation process. They let teams figure out how well the OKRs are being used and where improvements can be made. Without retrospectives, teams may not be able to learn from their experiences and improve the OKR process in the future.

Not having a clear understanding of what OKRs are. OKRs are a powerful tool for aligning teams and individuals around specific, measurable goals. However, if the organization does not have a clear understanding of what OKRs are, they may not be able to use them effectively.

Not having a plan for how to implement OKRs. OKRs can be an effective tool for aligning teams and individuals around common goals. However, if the organization does not have a plan for how to implement OKRs, they may not be able to use them effectively.

It is worth noting that each company has its own specific culture and needs; therefore, the mistakes could vary, but the above list is a common list of mistakes that could occur while implementing OKRs in a company.

Final word

Thank you for coming along with me to learn about the OKR method for goal setting. I hope you have gained valuable insights and strategies to help you set and achieve your goals more effectively.

Remember, the OKR method is a powerful tool that can help you focus on what's most important, eliminate distractions, and maximize your time and resources. By setting ambitious, goals and regularly tracking your progress, you can stay on track and achieve your goals with tremendous success. But it's important to go into the process of implementation with a clear understanding of the company's needs and culture. By following the steps in this book, companies can make sure that their teams and individuals are all working toward the same goals and that they can track their progress toward reaching these goals.

It is important to remember that OKRs are a living document and should be reviewed and updated regularly. By conducting regular check-ins and retrospectives and planning for the next quarter's OKRs, companies can ensure that they are continuously improving the OKR process.

It is also important to note that OKRs are not a one-size-fits-all solution; each company has its own specific culture, size, and needs; therefore, the implementation process should be tailored accordingly.

Please apply the principles and techniques you've learned in this book to your goals and watch the results come in. Whether you are looking to improve your productivity or lead a team to new heights, the OKR method can help you achieve your full potential.

Thank you for being a part of this book. I hope the best for you as you set and achieve your goals with the OKR method.

I would be glad to hear from you in my LinkedIn- https://www.linkedin.com/in/kkoptelov/ or see you at my courses or help you as a client in the OKR implementation project. For more details, please check my site https://www.okr.how and https://koptelov.org

www.ingramcontent.com/pod-product-compliance
Lightning Source LLC
Chambersburg PA
CBHW052351220526
45465CB00003BA/1052